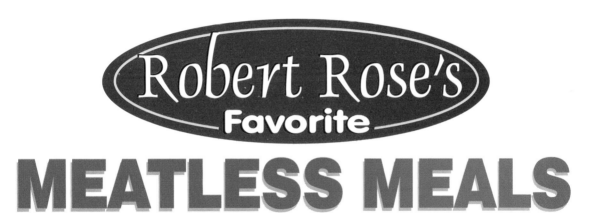

Robert Rose's Favorite

MEATLESS MEALS

D0939445

Robert
ROSE

ROBERT ROSE'S FAVORITE MEATLESS MEALS

Canadian Cataloguing in Publication Data

Main entry under title:

Robert Rose's favorite meatless meals

Includes index.

ISBN 1-896503-67-5

1. Vegetarian cookery.   I. Title: Favorite meatless meals.

TX837.R623 1998   641.5'636   C98-931530-4

DESIGN AND PAGE COMPOSITION: MATTHEWS COMMUNICATIONS DESIGN
PHOTOGRAPHY: MARK T. SHAPIRO

Cover photo: (INDIVIDUAL VEGETABLE GOAT CHEESE PIE, PAGE 45)

Distributed in the U.S. by: Distributed in Canada by:
Firefly Books (U.S.) Inc.   Stoddart Publishing Co. Ltd.
P.O. Box 1338   34 Lesmill Road
Ellicott Station   North York, Ontario
Buffalo, NY   14205   M3B 2T6

ORDER LINES   ORDER LINES
Tel: (416) 499-8412   Tel: (416) 213-1919
Fax: (416) 499-8313   Fax: (416) 213-1917

Published by: Robert Rose Inc. • 156 Duncan Mill Road, Suite 12
                  Toronto, Ontario, Canada M3B 2N2   Tel: (416) 449-3535

Printed in Canada   1234567 BP 01 00 99 98

About this book

At Robert Rose, we're committed to finding imaginative and exciting ways to provide our readers with cookbooks that offer great recipes — and exceptional value. That's the thinking behind our "Robert Rose's Favorite" series.

Here we've selected over 50 favorite meatless recipes from a number of our bestselling full-sized cookbooks: Byron Ayanoglu's *The New Vegetarian Gourmet* and *Simply Mediterranean Cooking*; Johanna Burkhard's *Comfort Food Cookbook*; Andrew Chase's *Asian Bistro Cookbook*; *New World Noodles* and *New World Chinese Cooking*, by Bill Jones and Stephen Wong; and Rose Reisman's *Light Cooking, Light Pasta, Enlightened Home Cooking* and *Light Vegetarian Cooking*.

We believe that it all adds up to great value for anyone who enjoys meatless meals.

Want to find out more about the sources of our recipes? See pages 94 and 95 for details.

Contents

Pasta and Grains

Desserts

Appetizers

Sautéed Vegetable Feta Cheese Spread

Serves 6 to 8

TIP

Pulse food processor on and off for a chunky texture.

Try goat cheese instead of feta.

For an attractive-looking spread, line a decorative mold with plastic wrap and unmold after chilled.

MAKE AHEAD

Prepare up to 2 days in advance.

**FROM
Rose Reisman's
Light Vegetarian Cooking**

1/2 cup	chopped carrots	125 mL
2 tsp	vegetable oil	10 mL
2 tsp	minced garlic	10 mL
3/4 cup	chopped red bell peppers	175 mL
3/4 cup	chopped leeks	175 mL
1/2 cup	chopped onions	125 mL
1/4 cup	sliced black olives	50 mL
2 tbsp	light sour cream	25 mL
2 tbsp	light mayonnaise	25 mL
1 tbsp	freshly squeezed lemon juice	15 mL
1/2 tsp	dried oregano	2 mL
2 oz	feta cheese, crumbled	50 g

1. Boil or steam carrots just until tender, about 5 minutes. Drain, and set aside.

2. In a saucepan, heat oil over medium-low heat. Add garlic, red peppers, leeks, onions and carrots; cook, stirring occasionally, for 5 minutes or until tender. Cool.

3. In a food processor, combine cooled vegetables, black olives, sour cream, mayonnaise, lemon juice, oregano and feta. Process to desired consistency. Serve with crackers or vegetables.

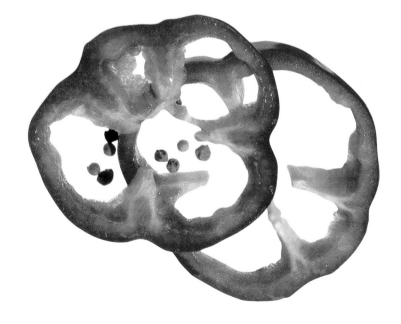

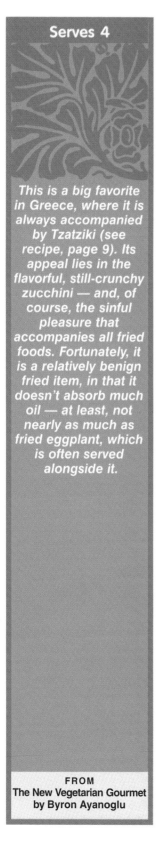

This is a big favorite in Greece, where it is always accompanied by Tzatziki (see recipe, page 9). Its appeal lies in the flavorful, still-crunchy zucchini — and, of course, the sinful pleasure that accompanies all fried foods. Fortunately, it is a relatively benign fried item, in that it doesn't absorb much oil — at least, not nearly as much as fried eggplant, which is often served alongside it.

FROM
The New Vegetarian Gourmet
by Byron Ayanoglu

Fried Zucchini

12 oz	zucchini (about 2 medium)	350 g
1 cup	all-purpose flour	250 mL
1/4 tsp	salt	2 mL
1/4 tsp	black pepper	2 mL
1/2 cup	vegetable oil	50 mL
1 cup	TZATZIKI SAUCE (see recipe, facing page) *or*	250 mL
4	lemon wedges	4

1. Trim stems of the zucchini. Slice lengthwise on the diagonal, about 1/4 inch (0.5 cm) thick, to obtain long, thin, elegant slices. Put in a bowl and add cold water to cover; let soak.

2. In another bowl, sift together the flour, salt and pepper. Place this bowl near the stove, along with the bowl containing the zucchini slices.

3. In a large frying pan, heat the oil over medium–high heat until it's just about to smoke. Working quickly, take a zucchini slice from the water, dredge thoroughly in the seasoned flour, and then put it into the hot oil. Repeat procedure until the pan is filled with a single layer of zucchini slices. Fry the slices for 2 minutes on one side until golden brown, but not burned; turn them over, using tongs if possible, and fry another 2 minutes.

4. Transfer the fried zucchini slices to a plate lined with a paper towel, then repeat dredging/frying procedure with any remaining slices. Once cooked, transfer all the zucchini slices to a plate. Serve immediately, accompanied by TZATZIKI SAUCE or lemon wedges.

Tzatziki Sauce

1/2 cup	peeled, coarsely shredded English cucumber	125 mL
1 cup	yogurt	250 mL
2	cloves garlic	2
	Salt to taste	
1 tsp	extra virgin olive oil	5 mL
Pinch	cayenne or paprika	Pinch

1. Drain cucumber through a strainer, pressing by hand to extract as much juice as possible (you can save this juice and use it as an astringent for the face).

2. In a bowl, stir together cucumber shreds and yogurt. Press garlic through a garlic press directly into bowl; mix in. Season to taste with salt.

3. Transfer sauce to a serving bowl and let rest for 30 minutes. Drizzle olive oil on it and sprinkle cayenne (for spicy) or paprika (for mild) just before serving.

Makes 1 1/3 cups
325 mL

A relative (and a descendant) of Afghani/Indian raitas, this soothing-yet-exciting yogurt-based sauce is a lovely complement to Greek-style fried zucchini and a wonderful dip for raw vegetables. In fact, you can use it to provide an additional taste sensation to any Mediterranean recipe. It's best when made ahead, and keeps nicely in the refrigerator for up to 3 days (after that it gets too garlicky). If refrigerated, it must be brought back up to room temperature.

FROM
The New Vegetarian Gourmet
by Byron Ayanoglu

Serves 6 to 8

TIP

Tired of garlic bread? This is a great alternative.

If fresh basil is not available, substitute parsley.

Roast your own red bell peppers or buy water-packed roasted red peppers.

Double recipe and use as a dip.

MAKE AHEAD

Prepare bean mixture up to 1 day in advance.

**FROM
Rose Reisman's
Light Vegetarian Cooking**

White Bean and Roasted Pepper Bruschetta

PREHEAT OVEN 425° F (220° C)
BAKING SHEET

1 cup	canned white kidney beans, rinsed and drained,	1
1/4 cup	chopped fresh basil (or 1/2 tsp [2 mL] dried)	50 mL
1 1/2 tsp	freshly squeezed lemon juice	7 mL
1/2 tsp	minced garlic	2 mL
1/2 tsp	sesame oil	2 mL
1	baguette or thin French loaf	1
2 tbsp	chopped roasted red peppers	25 mL

1. In a food processor, purée beans, basil, lemon juice, garlic and sesame oil until smooth.

2. Slice baguette into 1-inch (2.5 cm) slices. In a toaster oven or under a preheated broiler, toast until golden; turn and toast opposite side. Spread each slice with approximately 1 1/2 tsp (7 mL) bean mixture. Top with chopped red peppers.

3. Bake until warm, approximately 5 minutes.

Creamy Spinach Dip

Makes 3 cups
750 mL

Here's a dip that's so much tastier than the ones made with salty soup mixes. Serve with vegetable dippers such as carrot, pepper, cucumber, celery, broccoli, fennel and cauliflower. I use any leftovers as a dressing for pasta or potato salads, or as a spread for sandwiches.

T I P

To grate lemon rind, use a zester to remove the rind in thin shreds and finely chop with knife. When lemons are bargain-priced, stock up for the future: Grate the rinds and squeeze the juice; place in separate containers and freeze.

To make a bread bowl for serving: Using a serrated knife, slice 2 inches (5 cm) off top of small (1 lb [500 g]) unsliced round whole wheat or sourdough bread. Hollow out loaf, reserving contents, leaving a shell about 1 inch (2.5 cm) thick. Spoon dip into bread bowl. Cut reserved bread into strips or cubes and serve along with vegetable dippers.

FROM
The Comfort Food Cookbook
by Johanna Burkhard

1 pkg	(10 oz [300 g]) fresh or frozen spinach	1
1 cup	crumbed feta cheese (about 4 oz [125 g])	250 mL
1/3 cup	chopped green onions	75 mL
1/4 cup	chopped fresh dill	50 mL
1	clove garlic, minced	1
1 tsp	grated lemon rind	5 mL
1 1/2 cups	sour cream (regular or light)	375 mL
1/2 cup	light mayonnaise	125 mL

1. Remove tough stem ends from fresh spinach; wash in cold water. Place spinach with moisture clinging to leaves in a large saucepan. Cook over high heat, stirring, until just wilted. (If using frozen spinach, remove packaging and place in a glass bowl; microwave at High, stirring twice, for 5 minutes or until completely defrosted.) Place spinach in a colander to drain. Squeeze out moisture by hand; wrap in a clean, dry towel and squeeze out excess moisture.

2. In a food processor, combine spinach, feta, onions, dill, garlic and lemon rind. Process until very finely chopped.

3. Add sour cream and mayonnaise; process, using on-off turns, just until combined. Transfer to a serving bowl, cover and refrigerate until ready to serve. Serve in a bread bowl (see Tip, at left), if desired, and accompany with vegetable dippers.

Serves 6

TIP

Use plum tomatoes if available — they have less liquid. Or you can remove the seeds from regular tomatoes.

If in a hurry, microwave potatoes. Each potato cooks in approximately 8 minutes at high power.

Goat cheese or another sharp cheese can replace feta.

MAKE AHEAD

Prepare entire filling and stuff potatoes early in the day. Bake an extra 5 minutes or until hot.

FROM
Rose Reisman's Enlightened Home Cooking

Greek Baked Stuffed Potatoes with Tomato, Olives and Cheese

PREHEAT OVEN TO 425° F (220° C)

3	medium baking potatoes	3
2 tsp	vegetable oil	10 mL
1 1/2 tsp	minced garlic	7 mL
2/3 cup	chopped green peppers	150 mL
1/2 cup	chopped red onions	125 mL
1 1/2 tsp	dried oregano	7 mL
2/3 cup	chopped fresh tomatoes	150 mL
1/3 cup	sliced black olives	75 mL
1/4 cup	chopped green onions (about 2 medium)	50 mL
1/4 cup	2% yogurt	50 mL
1/4 cup	2% milk	50 mL
1 1/2 oz	feta cheese, crumbled	40 g

1. Bake the potatoes for 45 minutes to 1 hour, or until easily pierced with the tip of a sharp knife.

2. Meanwhile, in a nonstick skillet, heat oil over medium heat. Add garlic, green peppers, red onions and oregano and cook for 7 minutes or until softened, stirring occasionally. Stir in tomatoes, black olives and green onions and cook 1 minute more. Remove from heat.

3. When potatoes are cool enough to handle, cut in half lengthwise and scoop out flesh, leaving shells intact. Place shells on baking sheet. Mash potato and add yogurt, milk and 1 oz (25 g) of the feta. Stir in vegetable mixture. Divide among potato skin shells, sprinkle with remaining feta and bake for 15 minutes, or until heated through.

Leek Mushroom Cheese Pâté

9- BY 5-INCH (2 L) LOAF PAN LINED WITH PLASTIC WRAP

2 tsp	vegetable oil	10 mL
1 1/2 tsp	minced garlic	7 mL
1 1/2 cups	chopped leeks	375 mL
1/2 cup	finely chopped carrots	125 mL
12 oz	oyster or regular mushrooms, thinly sliced	375 g
2 tbsp	sherry or white wine	25 mL
2 tbsp	chopped fresh dill (or 2 tsp [10 mL] dried)	25 mL
1 1/2 tsp	dried oregano	7 mL
1/4 tsp	coarsely ground black pepper	1 mL
2 oz	feta cheese, crumbled	50 g
2 oz	light cream cheese	50 g
1/2 cup	5% ricotta cheese	125 mL
2 tsp	freshly squeezed lemon juice	10 mL
2 tbsp	chopped fresh dill	25 mL

1. In a large nonstick frying pan sprayed with vegetable spray, heat oil over medium-high heat. Add garlic, leeks and carrots; cook 3 minutes, stirring occasionally. Stir in mushrooms, sherry, dill, oregano and pepper; cook, stirring occasionally, 8 to 10 minutes or until carrots are tender and liquid is absorbed. Remove from heat.

2. Transfer vegetable mixture to a food processor. Add feta, cream cheese, ricotta and lemon juice; purée until smooth. Spoon into prepared loaf pan. Cover and chill until firm.

3. Invert onto serving platter; sprinkle with chopped dill. Serve with crackers, bread or vegetables.

Soups

Serves 4 to 6

TIP

Try grilling or barbecuing corn on the cob until charred. Remove kernels with a knife.

Fresh basil as a garnish is excellent.

Great soup in just under 30 minutes.

MAKE AHEAD

Prepare up to 2 days in advance. Add more stock if necessary when reheating.

Freeze for up to 3 weeks.

FROM
**Rose Reisman's
Light Vegetarian Cooking**

Corn, Tomato and Zucchini Soup

2 tsp	vegetable oil	10 mL
1 tsp	minced garlic	5 mL
3 cups	diced zucchini	750 mL
1 1/2 cups	chopped onions	375 mL
3 cups	vegetable stock	750 mL
1	can (19 oz [540 mL]) whole tomatoes	1
1 1/4 cups	frozen or canned corn, drained	300 mL
2 tsp	dried basil	10 mL

1. In a nonstick saucepan sprayed with vegetable spray, heat oil over medium–high heat. Add garlic, zucchini and onions; cook for 5 minutes or until softened.

2. Stir in stock, tomatoes, corn, and basil. Bring to a boil, reduce heat to low and simmer 20 minutes, breaking up whole tomatoes with the back of a spoon.

Serves 4 to 6

TIP

Buy cauliflower with bright, light-colored heads and tightly packed florets.

For a stronger taste, use aged Cheddar or Swiss cheese.

MAKE AHEAD

Prepare and refrigerate up to a day before and reheat before serving, adding more stock if too thick.

Cauliflower Potato Soup

1 tbsp	vegetable oil	15 mL
1 tsp	crushed garlic	5 mL
1 cup	chopped onions	250 mL
1	medium cauliflower, separated into florets	1
4 cups	chicken stock	1 L
2	small potatoes, peeled and chopped	2
1/4 cup	shredded Cheddar cheese	50 mL
2 tbsp	chopped fresh chives	25 mL

1. In large nonstick saucepan, heat oil; sauté garlic and onions until softened, approximately 5 minutes.

2. Add cauliflower, stock and potatoes; bring to boil. Cover, reduce heat and simmer for 25 minutes or until tender. Transfer to food processor and purée until creamy and smooth. Return to saucepan and thin with more stock if desired.

3. Ladle into bowls; sprinkle with cheese and chives.

FROM
Rose Reisman Brings
Home Light Cooking

Tortellini Minestrone with Spinach

2 tsp	vegetable oil	10 mL
2 tsp	minced garlic	10 mL
1 cup	chopped onions	250 mL
1/2 cup	chopped carrots	125 mL
1/2 cup	chopped celery	125 mL
4 cups	vegetable stock	1 L
1 tsp	dried basil	5 mL
1/4 tsp	freshly ground black pepper	1 mL
1 1/2 cups	diced plum tomatoes	375 mL
2 cups	chopped fresh spinach	500 mL
2 cups	frozen cheese tortellini	500 mL
3 tbsp	grated Parmesan cheese	45 mL

1. In a nonstick saucepan sprayed with vegetable spray, heat oil over medium-high heat. Add garlic, onions, carrots and celery; cook 4 minutes or until onions are softened.

2. Add stock, basil and pepper. Bring to a boil; reduce heat to medium and cook 8 minutes or until vegetables are tender-crisp.

3. Stir in tomatoes, spinach and tortellini. Cover and cook 5 minutes or until tortellini is heated through and vegetables are tender. Serve immediately, garnished with Parmesan cheese.

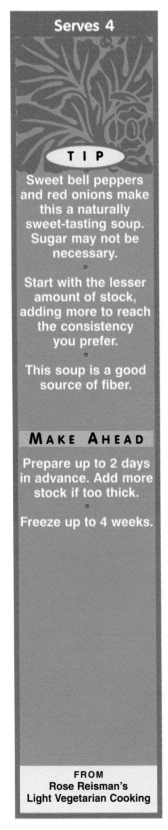

Serves 4

TIP

Sweet bell peppers and red onions make this a naturally sweet-tasting soup. Sugar may not be necessary.

Start with the lesser amount of stock, adding more to reach the consistency you prefer.

This soup is a good source of fiber.

MAKE AHEAD

Prepare up to 2 days in advance. Add more stock if too thick.

Freeze up to 4 weeks.

FROM
Rose Reisman's
Light Vegetarian Cooking

Red Onion and Grilled Red Pepper Soup

PREHEAT OVEN TO BROIL
BAKING SHEET

3	large red bell peppers	3
2 tsp	vegetable oil	10 mL
2 tsp	minced garlic	10 mL
1 tbsp	packed brown sugar	15 mL
5 cups	thinly sliced red onions	1.25 L
3 to 3 1/2 cups	vegetable stock	750 mL to 875 mL

Garnish

1/3 cup	chopped fresh basil or parsley	75 mL
	Light sour cream (optional)	

1. Arrange oven rack 6 inches (15 cm) under element. Cook peppers on baking sheet, turning occasionally, 20 minutes or until charred. Cool. Discard stem, skin and seeds; cut peppers into thin strips. Set aside.

2. In a large nonstick saucepan, heat oil over medium-low heat. Add garlic, brown sugar and red onions; cook, stirring occasionally, 15 minutes or until onions are browned. Stir in stock and red pepper strips; cook 15 minutes longer.

3. In a blender or food processor, purée soup until smooth. Serve hot, garnished with chopped basil or parsley and a dollop of sour cream, if desired.

Salads

Serves 4 to 6

T I P

Julienned carrots make a great substitute for the bean sprouts; blanch before using.

Toast sesame seeds in nonstick skillet over high heat for 2 to 3 minutes.

Substitute other vegetables of your choice.

MAKE AHEAD

Prepare salad and dressing earlier in the day. Keep separate in refrigerator until ready to serve.

FROM
Rose Reisman's
Light Vegetarian Cooking

Oriental Vegetable Salad

2 1/2 cups	trimmed green beans	625 mL
2 cups	asparagus cut into 1-inch (2.5 cm) pieces	500 mL
1 1/2 cups	halved snow peas	375 mL
1 3/4 cups	bean sprouts	425 mL
1 1/2 cups	sliced red bell peppers	375 mL
1 cup	chopped baby corn cobs	250 mL
3/4 cup	canned sliced water chestnuts, drained	175 mL
3/4 cup	canned mandarin oranges, drained	175 mL

Dressing

4 tsp	soya sauce	20 mL
4 tsp	rice wine vinegar	20 mL
1 tbsp	olive oil	15 mL
1 tbsp	honey	15 mL
2 tsp	sesame oil	10 mL
2 tsp	toasted sesame seeds	10 mL
1 1/2 tsp	minced garlic	7 mL
1 tsp	minced ginger root	5 mL

1. Boil or steam green beans and asparagus for 2 to 3 minutes or until tender-crisp; drain. Rinse under cold water and drain; transfer to a large serving bowl.

2. Boil or steam snow peas 45 seconds or until tender-crisp; drain. Rinse under cold water and drain; add to serving bowl along with bean sprouts, red peppers, corn cobs, water chestnuts and mandarin oranges. Toss to combine.

3. In a small bowl, whisk together soya sauce, vinegar, olive oil, honey, sesame oil, sesame seeds, garlic and ginger. Pour over salad; toss to coat.

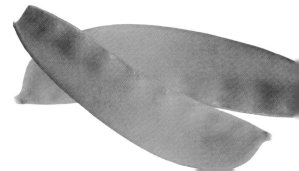

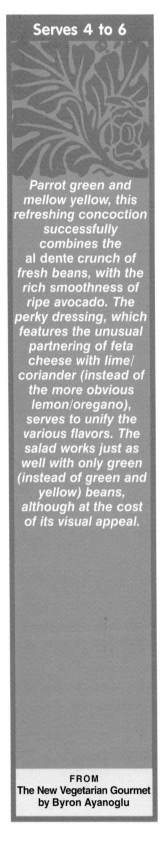

Parrot green and mellow yellow, this refreshing concoction successfully combines the al dente crunch of fresh beans, with the rich smoothness of ripe avocado. The perky dressing, which features the unusual partnering of feta cheese with lime/coriander (instead of the more obvious lemon/oregano), serves to unify the various flavors. The salad works just as well with only green (instead of green and yellow) beans, although at the cost of its visual appeal.

FROM
**The New Vegetarian Gourmet
by Byron Ayanoglu**

Green and Yellow Salad

1/2 lb	fresh green beans, trimmed	250 g
1/2 lb	fresh yellow beans, trimmed	250 g
1 tbsp	lime juice	15 mL
1	ripe avocado	1
	Salt and pepper to taste	
3 tbsp	olive oil	45 mL
3	green onions, finely chopped	3
4 oz	feta cheese, crumbled in large chunks	125 g
	Few sprigs fresh coriander, roughly chopped	

1. Boil green and yellow beans over high heat for 5 to 7 minutes. Drain and immediately refresh in a bowl of ice-cold water. Drain, and put in a wide salad bowl.

2. Put lime juice in a bowl. Peel avocado and cut into slices (or scoop out with a small spoon), and add to the lime juice. Fold avocado into the juice until well coated. Scatter avocado slices (or scoops) decoratively over the beans, along with any leftover lime juice. Season to taste with salt and pepper.

3. Drizzle olive oil over salad, and garnish with chopped green onions. Distribute feta over the salad, and top with a scattering of the chopped coriander. The salad can wait up to 1 hour, covered and unrefrigerated.

Serves 4 to 6

TIP

This dressing can also be used on other salads, such as mesclun mix, blanched asparagus, or even simple grated carrots. For special occasions, add grilled seafood such as prawns or scallops.

Vegetable Salad with Honey Sesame Soya Vinaigrette

2 cups	sliced blanched snow peas	500 mL
1 cup	carrots, cut into matchsticks	250 mL
1 cup	jicama, cut into matchsticks	250 mL
	or sliced water chestnuts	

Dressing

2 tsp	sesame oil	10 mL
2 tbsp	rice vinegar	25 mL
1 tbsp	fresh lemon juice	15 mL
2 tbsp	soya sauce	25 mL
2 tsp	honey	10 mL
1/4 cup	canola oil	50 mL
1 tsp	grated ginger root	5 mL
2 tsp	finely chopped chives	10 mL
2 tsp	toasted sesame seeds (equal parts black and white seeds, if desired)	10 mL
1 tsp	chili flakes (optional)	5 mL
1 tbsp	chopped cilantro	15 mL

1. In a serving bowl, combine snow peas, carrots and jicama or water chestnuts; toss to mix.

2. In a glass jar, combine ingredients for dressing; shake well. Toss with salad. Sprinkle with cilantro and serve.

FROM
New World Chinese Cooking
by Bill Jones & Stephen Wong

Serves 4 to 6

These marinated beets live in the fridge for up to a week, providing a healthy and ever-more-flavorful side course at a moment's notice. The onion and garlic are cut thick so that they can be avoided by those on a heavy date. The old problem with beets is that they turn everything that touches them (hands, cutting board) a royal purple. Fortunately, it washes off.

FROM
The New Vegetarian Gourmet
by Byron Ayanoglu

Garlic Beets

1 lb	beets, unpeeled but well scrubbed	500 g
4	cloves garlic, coarsely chopped	4
1/3 cup	thickly sliced red onion	75 mL
2 tbsp	red wine vinegar	25 mL
3 tbsp	extra virgin olive oil	45 mL
	Salt and pepper to taste	
	Few sprigs fresh coriander and/or parsley, chopped	

1. Place beets in a large saucepan and add enough water to cover by 1 1/2 inches (3 cm). Bring to boil and cook beets until they can be pierced easily with a fork, about 50 to 60 minutes. If water evaporates to expose beets during cooking, replenish with more hot water.

2. Drain beets, reserving cooking liquid. Let the beets cool for about 20 minutes, then peel them (the skins should slip right off). With a sharp knife, trim the beets' tops and bottoms, as well as any small blemishes.

3. Slice beets into rounds 1/4 inch (0.5 cm) thick. Transfer slices to a bowl and add garlic and onions. Sprinkle evenly with the wine vinegar and fold the mixture gently until well combined. Add olive oil and 1/2 cup (125 mL) of the reserved cooking liquid. (Discard the rest of the liquid.) Mix well. Season to taste with salt and pepper and let rest for at least 20 minutes.

4. Transfer beet mixture to a serving bowl. Toss a few times, garnish with the herb(s) and serve.

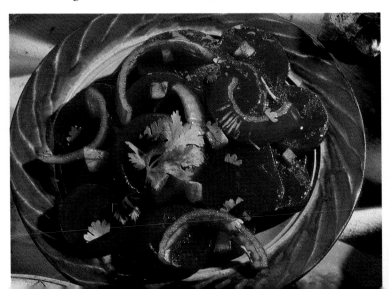

Serves 4 to 6

T I P

Sweet fruit and a combination of lettuces make this a perfect salad.

•

Any ripe fruit can replace pears.

•

If you don't care for the bitter flavor of curly endive and radicchio, use romaine or Bibb lettuce instead.

•

If you don't want the salad to wilt, use a larger amount of romaine lettuce.

M A K E A H E A D

Prepare salad and dressing early in the day. Toss just before serving.

FROM
Rose Reisman's
Light Vegetarian Cooking

Pear, Lettuce and Feta Cheese Salad

Dressing

2 tbsp	raspberry vinegar	25 mL
2 1/2 tbsp	olive oil	35 mL
1 tsp	minced garlic	5 mL
1 1/2 tsp	honey	7 mL
1 tsp	sesame oil	5 mL

Salad

4 cups	red or green leaf lettuce, washed, dried and torn into pieces	1 L
1 1/2 cups	curly endive or escarole, washed, dried and torn into pieces	375 mL
1 1/2 cups	radicchio, washed, dried and torn into pieces	375 mL
1 cup	diced pears (about 1 pear)	250 mL
2 oz	feta cheese, crumbled	50 g
1/3 cup	sliced black olives	75 mL

1. Prepare the dressing: In a small bowl, whisk together vinegar, olive oil, garlic, honey and sesame oil; set aside.

2. Make the salad: In a serving bowl, combine leaf lettuce, curly endive, radicchio, pears, feta and olives. Pour dressing over; toss gently to coat. Serve immediately.

Serves 4 to 6

Yard-long beans are available virtually year-round in Asian food markets. They look like green beans but are slender and measure a foot and a half in length. If they aren't available, green beans, yellow wax beans, sugar snap peas and asparagus all work well with this dressing.

T I P

If fresh mandarin oranges aren't available, use the canned variety. To make mandarin orange juice: Drain and purée in a blender until liquefied.

For an interesting garnish, try adding CANDIED PECANS (see recipe page 30). They will add delicious texture to the salad.

FROM
New World Chinese Cooking
by Bill Jones & Stephen Wong

Yard-Long Bean Salad with Purple Onions in Mustard Mandarin Orange Dressing

Dressing

2 tbsp	Dijon mustard	25 mL
2 tsp	Chinese black vinegar *or* rice vinegar	10 mL
1 tsp	mandarin orange zest *or* orange zest	5 mL
1/2 cup	canola oil	125 mL
1/4 cup	mandarin orange juice (see note, at left)	50 mL
2 tsp	chopped fresh mint	10 mL
Pinch	granulated sugar	Pinch
	Salt and pepper to taste	
1 lb	yard-long beans (or green beans or a combination of green and yellow wax beans), trimmed and cut into 2-inch (5 cm) long pieces	500 g
2	small purple onions, sliced	2
1 tsp	finely chopped garlic	5 mL
1/2 cup	CANDIED PECANS (optional) (see recipe, page 30)	125 mL

1. In a mixing bowl, combine mustard, vinegar and orange zest ; mix well. Add oil in a slow stream, whisking constantly, until emulsified. Add orange juice; mix well. Fold in mint. Adjust seasoning with sugar, salt and pepper. Set aside.

2. In a large pot of salted boiling water, blanch beans until tender-crisp, about 2 minutes. (If using green or wax beans, blanch for 4 minutes or until tender-crisp.) Remove from heat; drain and cool thoroughly by plunging into ice water. Drain and pat dry with paper towels.

3. In a serving bowl, combine beans, onions, garlic and dressing; toss until vegetables are well coated. Let stand for 5 to 10 minutes. Garnish with CANDIED PECANS, if desired, and serve.

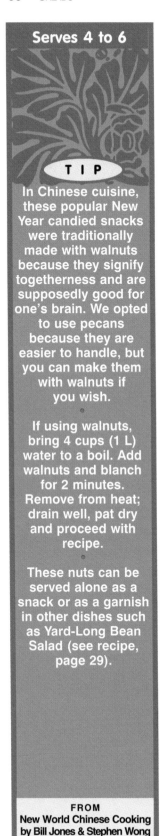

Serves 4 to 6

T I P

In Chinese cuisine, these popular New Year candied snacks were traditionally made with walnuts because they signify togetherness and are supposedly good for one's brain. We opted to use pecans because they are easier to handle, but you can make them with walnuts if you wish.

·

If using walnuts, bring 4 cups (1 L) water to a boil. Add walnuts and blanch for 2 minutes. Remove from heat; drain well, pat dry and proceed with recipe.

·

These nuts can be served alone as a snack or as a garnish in other dishes such as Yard-Long Bean Salad (see recipe, page 29).

FROM
New World Chinese Cooking
by Bill Jones & Stephen Wong

Baked Candied Pecans

PREHEAT OVEN TO 275° F (140° C)
BAKING SHEET SPRAYED WITH VEGETABLE SPRAY

1 lb	shelled raw pecan or walnut halves	500 g
1 cup	water	250 mL
1 cup	sugar	250 mL
1/2 cup	honey	125 mL
1/4 tsp	salt	1 mL
2 tbsp	toasted sesame seeds (optional)	25 mL

1. In large skillet, combine water, sugar, honey and salt. Bring to a boil; cook until liquid coats the back of a spoon with the consistency of corn syrup. Reduce heat to medium. Add nuts; stir and boil for about 1 minute, making sure that nuts are well coated.

2. With a slotted spoon, transfer nuts to prepared baking sheet. (Be sure to separate and spread them out evenly.) Bake 20 to 25 minutes or until golden brown, turning once.

3. Remove from oven and cool slightly. If you want to eat the nuts as a snack, while they're still warm and sticky, toss them in a mixing bowl with sesame seeds. Spread out coated nuts again on baking sheet sheet; let cool and harden thoroughly. Store in a glass jar with a tight-fitting lid.

Serves 12 as an accompaniment

This is a famous pickle from northern China. The spiced Napa cabbage is soured naturally at room temperature; it will continue to sour slowly in the refrigerator and is best eaten within a few days. Szechuan peppercorns are essential for this recipe; they are available at all Chinese (and some Asian) grocers or, occasionally, in the spice sections of supermarkets.

FROM
The Asian Bistro Cookbook
by Andrew Chase

Chinese Spicy Pickled Napa Cabbage

1	medium Napa cabbage, about 2 lbs (1 kg)	1
2 tbsp	salt (preferably sea salt)	25 mL
1 tsp	Szechuan peppercorns	5 mL
4 to 8	whole small dried red chilies	4 to 8
1 tbsp	julienned ginger root	15 mL
2	garlic cloves, thinly sliced (optional)	2

1. Cut Napa cabbage into sixths, core and slice across each section into 2-inch (5 cm) wide sections; mix well with salt. Cover; set aside at room temperature for 1 day in warm weather or 2 in cooler weather (taste after 1 day to see if the cabbage has soured). Rinse lightly under cold running water; drain, squeezing out excess moisture. Set aside.

2. In a dry frying pan over medium heat, toast Szechuan peppercorns until fragrant and slightly darkened. Toast chilies until fragrant and slightly darker in color. Stir together cabbage, Szechuan peppercorns, chilies, ginger and garlic (if using), pressing with your hands to extract liquid from cabbage and to break up the chilies. Cover; refrigerate 1 day before serving.

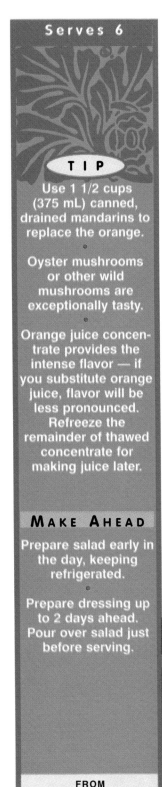

TIP

Use 1 1/2 cups (375 mL) canned, drained mandarins to replace the orange.

Oyster mushrooms or other wild mushrooms are exceptionally tasty.

Orange juice concentrate provides the intense flavor — if you substitute orange juice, flavor will be less pronounced. Refreeze the remainder of thawed concentrate for making juice later.

MAKE AHEAD

Prepare salad early in the day, keeping refrigerated.

Prepare dressing up to 2 days ahead. Pour over salad just before serving.

FROM
Rose Reisman's Enlightened
Home Cooking

Spinach Salad with Oranges and Mushrooms

8 cups	packed fresh spinach leaves, washed, dried and torn into bite-sized pieces	2 L
1 1/2 cups	sliced mushrooms	375 mL
3/4 cup	sliced water chestnuts	175 mL
1/2 cup	sliced red onions	125 mL
1/4 cup	raisins	50 mL
2 tbsp	sliced or chopped almonds, toasted	25 mL
1	orange, peeled and sections cut into pieces	1

Dressing

3 tbsp	olive oil	45 mL
3 tbsp	balsamic vinegar	45 mL
2 tbsp	orange juice concentrate, thawed	25 mL
1 tbsp	honey	15 mL
1 tsp	grated orange zest	5 mL
1 tsp	minced garlic	5 mL

1. In large serving bowl, combine spinach, mushrooms, water chestnuts, red onions, raisins, almonds and orange pieces; toss well.

2. In small bowl, whisk together olive oil, balsamic vinegar, orange juice concentrate, honey, orange zest and garlic; pour over salad and toss.

Main and Side Dishes

Potato Crust Pesto Pizza

PREHEAT OVEN TO 425° F (220° C)
10-INCH (3 L) SPRINGFORM PAN SPRAYED
WITH VEGETABLE SPRAY

3 cups	diced potatoes	750 mL
2 tbsp	olive oil	25 mL
1 cup	all-purpose flour	250 mL
2 tbsp	grated Parmesan cheese	25 mL
1 tsp	dried basil	5 mL
1/4 tsp	salt	1 mL
1/4 tsp	freshly ground black pepper	1 mL
1/3 cup	CREAMY PESTO SAUCE (see below)	75 mL
1/4 cup	sliced black olives	50 mL
1/4 cup	thinly sliced red bell peppers	50 mL
1/2 cup	shredded part-skim mozzarella cheese (about 2 oz [50 g])	125 mL

1. In a saucepan, add cold water to cover potatoes. Bring to a boil; cook 10 minutes or until tender when pierced with the tip of a knife. Drain; mash with oil. Stir in flour, Parmesan, basil, salt and pepper until well mixed. Do not overmix. Press onto bottom of prepared pan. Bake 15 minutes or until golden at edges.

2. Spread with pesto. Sprinkle with black olives, red peppers and mozzarella. Return to oven; bake 10 minutes.

Creamy Pesto Sauce

1 cup	fresh packed basil	250 mL
1/4 cup	light sour cream	50 mL
2 tbsp	light mayonnaise	25 mL
1 1/2 tbsp	grated Parmesan cheese	22 mL
1 tbsp	olive oil	15 mL
1 tbsp	toasted pine nuts	15 mL
1 1/2 tsp	freshly squeezed lemon juice	7 mL
1 tsp	minced garlic	5 mL

1. In a food processor, combine basil, sour cream, mayonnaise, Parmesan, oil, pine nuts, lemon juice and garlic; process until smooth.

Mashed White and Sweet Potato Casserole

PREHEAT OVEN TO 400° F (200° C)
8-INCH SQUARE (2 L) CASSEROLE DISH
SPRAYED WITH VEGETABLE SPRAY

2 tsp	vegetable oil	10 mL
2 tsp	minced garlic	10 mL
1 cup	chopped onions	250 mL
1 lb	potatoes, peeled and quartered	500 g
2/3 cup	5% ricotta cheese	150 mL
1/4 cup	light sour cream	50 mL
1/4 cup	2% milk	50 mL
1/4 cup	finely chopped red or green peppers	50 mL
3 tbsp	fresh chopped dill (or 1 tsp [5 mL] dried)	45 mL
1 lb	sweet potatoes, peeled and quartered	500 g
1/2 cup	2% milk	125 mL
1/4 cup	chopped sun-dried tomatoes	50 mL
1/4 cup	chopped green onions (about 2 medium)	50 mL
3 tbsp	bread crumbs	45 mL
1 oz	goat cheese	25 g
1 tsp	margarine or butter	5 mL

1. In small nonstick skillet, heat oil over medium heat. Cook garlic and onions for 4 minutes, or until softened. Divide mixture in half.

2. Put potatoes in saucepan with cold water to cover; bring to a boil and cook for 15 minutes, or until tender when pierced with the tip of a knife. Drain and mash with ricotta, sour cream and milk; stir in red peppers, dill and half of onion mixture.

3. Put sweet potatoes in saucepan with cold water to cover; bring to a boil and cook for 10 minutes or until tender when pierced with the tip of a knife. Drain and mash with milk; stir in sun-dried tomatoes and green onions. Place mixture to one side of casserole dish, and put mashed white potato mixture to the other side.

4. In small bowl, combine bread crumbs, goat cheese and margarine; sprinkle over top of casserole. Bake for 15 minutes, uncovered, or until heated through.

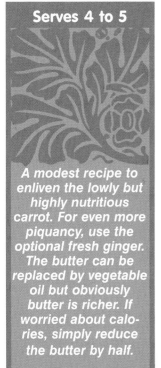

Serves 4 to 5

A modest recipe to enliven the lowly but highly nutritious carrot. For even more piquancy, use the optional fresh ginger. The butter can be replaced by vegetable oil but obviously butter is richer. If worried about calories, simply reduce the butter by half.

Caraway Carrots

3 cups	diagonally sliced carrots	750 mL
1 tsp	cornstarch	5 mL
1 tbsp	cold water	15 mL
2 tbsp	butter	25 mL
1 tbsp	whole caraway seeds	15 mL
1 tsp	grated ginger root (optional)	5 mL
1 tbsp	honey, maple syrup or brown sugar	15 mL
1 tbsp	lemon juice	15 mL
2	green onions, finely chopped	2

1. In a saucepan, cover carrot slices with cold water. Bring to a boil; cook 2 to 4 minutes, depending on desired tenderness. Drain carrots, reserving the cooking water.

2. In a small bowl, stir together the cornstarch and the 1 tbsp (15 mL) water until dissolved.

3. In a deep saucepan, heat butter over medium heat until bubbling, about 1 or 2 minutes. Add caraway seeds and stir-fry for 1 to 2 minutes until the seeds begin to pop. Add 1/2 cup (125 mL) of the reserved cooking water, the ginger (if using) and the honey; cook, stirring occasionally, for 2 to 3 minutes, until nearly boiling. Stir dissolved cornstarch and add to sauce; reduce heat to low and cook, stirring, for 2 to 3 minutes until the sauce has the consistency of a thin syrup.

4. Fold carrots into the sauce and cook for 2 to 3 minutes until heated through. Remove from heat and stir in lemon juice. Transfer to a serving dish and garnish with green onions. Serve immediately.

FROM
The New Vegetarian Gourmet
by Byron Ayanoglu

Carrot Roll with Artichoke Garlic Filling

PREHEAT OVEN TO 350° F (180° C)
15- BY 10-INCH (37.5 BY 25 CM) JELLY ROLL PAN LINED WITH PARCHMENT PAPER AND SPRAYED WITH VEGETABLE SPRAY

Roll

2 cups	diced carrots	500 mL
2	egg yolks	2
1/3 cup	chopped fresh dill (or 2 tsp [10 mL] dried)	75 mL
1/3 cup	all-purpose flour	75 mL
3 tbsp	light sour cream	45 mL
1 1/2 tbsp	packed brown sugar	22 mL
4	egg whites	4
Pinch	salt	Pinch
2 tsp	dry bread crumbs	10 mL

Filling

Half	can (14 oz [398 mL]) artichoke hearts, drained	Half
1/2 cup	5% smooth ricotta cheese	125 mL
3 tbsp	light sour cream	45 mL
3 tbsp	chopped green onions	45 mL
1 1/2 tbsp	grated Parmesan cheese	20 mL
1/2 tsp	minced garlic	2 mL

1. Boil or steam carrots until tender; rinse under cold water and drain. Add carrots, yolks, dill, flour, sour cream and brown sugar to food processor; purée. Transfer to a large bowl.

2. In a separate bowl using an electric mixer, beat egg whites with salt until stiff peaks form. Stir one-quarter of egg whites into carrot mixture. Fold in remaining egg whites. Spoon onto prepared jelly roll pan and smooth top with spatula. Bake 10 to 12 minutes. Let cool 5 minutes. Sprinkle evenly with 1 tsp (5 mL) of the bread crumbs.

3. Invert jelly roll pan onto a clean tea towel. Remove pan and gently remove parchment paper. Sprinkle with remaining 1 tsp (5 mL) bread crumbs. Roll up carrot roll along short end in tea towel. Allow to cool completely.

4. Meanwhile, make the filling: In a food processor, purée artichoke hearts, ricotta, sour cream, green onions, Parmesan and garlic until smooth.

5. Unroll carrot roll. Spread with artichoke filling and tightly re-roll. Serve at room temperature. Cut into 1-inch (2.5 cm) slices with a serrated knife.

Serves 4

TIP

Smaller carrots are more tender and sweeter than larger ones.

Green beans can be a good substitute for snow peas.

Walnuts or pine nuts can replace pecans.

Toast pecans in small skillet on stove for 2 minutes or in 400° F (200° C) oven until golden.

FROM
Rose Reisman Brings
Home Light Cooking

Carrots and Snow Peas with Maple Syrup and Pecans

1/2 lb	carrots, sliced thinly	250 g
1/2 lb	snow peas	250 g
1 1/2 tsp	margarine	7 mL
3 tbsp	maple syrup	45 mL
2 tbsp	chopped fresh parsley	25 mL
2 tbsp	chopped pecans, toasted	25 mL
1/2 tsp	cinnamon	2 mL

1. Steam or microwave carrots at High just until barely tender, approximately 2 minutes. Drain and set aside.

2. Steam or microwave snow peas just until barely tender, approximately 2 minutes. Drain and set aside.

3. In nonstick skillet, heat margarine and maple syrup. Add carrots, snow peas and parsley; cook for 1 minute. Serve sprinkled with pecans and cinnamon.

Serves 4 to 6

T I P

Feta cheese, grated Cheddar or Swiss can replace goat cheese. A stronger tasting cheese suits this dish.

Either use bottled-in-water roasted red peppers or, under a broiler, roast a small pepper for 15 to 20 minutes or until charred. Cool, then peel, deseed and chop. Use remainder for another purpose.

M AKE A HEAD

Prepare entire dish early in the day. Bake just before serving.

FROM
**Rose Reisman's
Enlightened Home Cooking**

Eggplant with Goat Cheese and Roasted Sweet Peppers

PREHEAT OVEN TO 350° F (180° C)
BAKING SHEET SPRAYED WITH VEGETABLE SPRAY

1	egg	1
1/4 cup	2% milk	50 mL
3/4 cup	seasoned bread crumbs	175 mL
2 tbsp	vegetable oil	25 mL
10	1/2-inch (1 cm) slices eggplant, skin on	10
3 oz	goat cheese	75 g
3 tbsp	2% milk	45 mL
3 tbsp	chopped roasted red peppers	45 mL
1/4 cup	chopped green onions (about 2 medium)	50 mL
1/2 tsp	minced garlic	2 mL

1. Beat egg and milk together in small bowl. Put bread crumbs on plate. Dip the eggplant slices in egg wash then press into bread crumbs. In large nonstick skillet sprayed with vegetable spray, heat 1 tbsp (15 mL) of the oil over medium heat. Add half of the breaded eggplant slices and cook for 4 minutes or until golden brown on both sides. Add remaining 1 tbsp (15 mL) oil and respray skillet with vegetable spray. Repeat with remaining eggplant slices. Place on prepared baking sheet.

2. In small bowl, stir together goat cheese, milk, red peppers, green onions and garlic. Put a spoonful of topping on top of each eggplant slice. Bake for 10 minutes or until heated through.

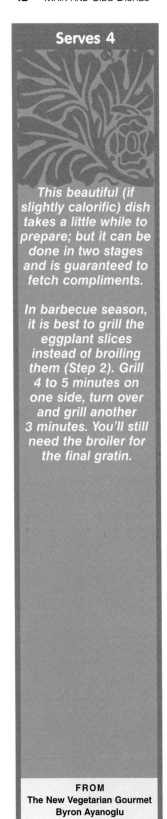

Serves 4

This beautiful (if slightly calorific) dish takes a little while to prepare; but it can be done in two stages and is guaranteed to fetch compliments.

In barbecue season, it is best to grill the eggplant slices instead of broiling them (Step 2). Grill 4 to 5 minutes on one side, turn over and grill another 3 minutes. You'll still need the broiler for the final gratin.

FROM
The New Vegetarian Gourmet
Byron Ayanoglu

Grilled Eggplant with Goat Cheese

PREHEAT BROILER AND, IF USING, START BARBECUE
BAKING SHEET

1	eggplant (about 1 lb [500 g])	1
1 tsp	salt	5 mL
2 tbsp	olive oil	25 mL
4 oz	soft goat cheese	125 g
1 tbsp	olive oil	15 mL
1 tbsp	balsamic vinegar	15 mL
1 tsp	drained capers	5 mL
	Black pepper to taste	
	Few sprigs fresh basil and/or parsley, chopped	

1. Cut off top 1/2 inch (1 cm) of the eggplant and discard. Slice 12 perfect round slices, about 1/4 inch (0.5 cm) thick. Sprinkle salt on both sides of the eggplant slices, and let rest 10 minutes.

2. Rinse salt off the slices and pat dry. Brush each side of slices with the olive oil. Lay them out on a baking sheet and broil them 6 to 7 minutes on the first side, until soft. Flip them, and broil the second side for 2 to 3 minutes.

3. Remove from broiler. Arrange eggplant slices on the baking sheet in 4 clusters of 3 slices each. Divide the cheese into 4 equal portions and form each into a patty; place one patty in the center of each cluster. Sprinkle each cluster evenly with the olive oil.

4. Return to the broiler and broil for 2 to 3 minutes until the cheese is melted and has started to brown a little.

5. With a spatula, carefully lift each cluster onto a plate. Sprinkle with the vinegar, capers, black pepper and chopped herb(s). Serve immediately.

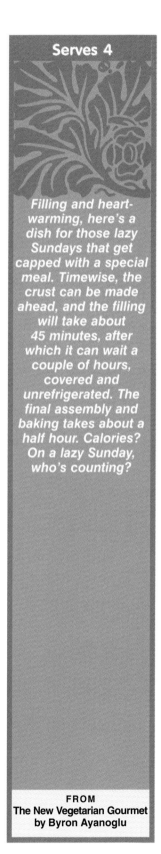

Serves 4

Filling and heart-warming, here's a dish for those lazy Sundays that get capped with a special meal. Timewise, the crust can be made ahead, and the filling will take about 45 minutes, after which it can wait a couple of hours, covered and unrefrigerated. The final assembly and baking takes about a half hour. Calories? On a lazy Sunday, who's counting?

FROM
The New Vegetarian Gourmet
by Byron Ayanoglu

Individual Vegetable Goat-Cheese Pie

PREHEAT OVEN TO 400° F (210° C)
4 RAMEKINS, 1 1/2 CUP (375 mL) CAPACITY, MEASURING
1 TO 2 INCHES (5 CM) DEEP AND 5 INCHES (12.5 CM) WIDE

1 lb	ripe tomatoes (about 4)	500 g
1/2 lb	potatoes, unpeeled but scrubbed	250 g
5 tbsp	olive oil	75 mL
1/2 tsp	salt	2 mL
1/2 tsp	black pepper	2 mL
2 1/2 cups	zucchini, thinly sliced	625 mL
1 1/2 cups	chopped onions	375 mL
1/2 cup	chopped green peppers	125 mL
3 cups	sliced mushrooms	750 mL
5	cloves garlic, finely chopped	5
1 tsp	dried oregano	5 mL
1 1/2 tsp	tomato paste	7 mL
3/4 cup	hot water	175 mL
4 oz	soft goat cheese	125 g
4	sheets OLIVE OIL CRUST (see recipe, page 47)	4
1	egg	1
1 tbsp	milk	15 mL

1. Blanch tomatoes in boiling water for 30 seconds. Over a bowl, peel, core and deseed them. Chop tomatoes roughly and set aside. Strain any accumulated tomato juices from bowl and add to tomato pieces.

2. Boil potato for 6 or 7 minutes, just until it can be pierced with a fork. Let cool for a few minutes, and cut into 1/2-inch (1 cm) cubes. Set aside.

3. In a large frying pan, heat 1/4 cup (50 mL) of the olive oil on high heat for 30 seconds. Add salt and pepper and stir for 30 seconds. Add potato cubes and fry, turning for 5 minutes, until browned and soft. Transfer potatoes to a bowl.

4. Put zucchini slices in the frying pan and fry, turning, for 3 or 4 minutes until browned. Remove zucchini and add to the reserved potatoes.

5. Heat the remaining olive oil. Add onions and green peppers; stir-fry for 2 to 3 minutes. Add mushrooms and stir-fry for 1 to 2 minutes. Add garlic and stir-fry for 1 to 2 minutes.

6. Add tomato flesh and juices and oregano to the pan. Stir-cook for 3 minutes to break up the tomato somewhat. Add the tomato paste diluted in hot water and lower heat to medium. Stir-cook 3 to 4 minutes, until everything is integrated and bubbling. Add the contents of the frying pan to the bowl with the potatoes and zucchini. Mix well to integrate.

7. Put one quarter of the vegetable mixture (about 1 1/4 cups [300 mL]) into each ramekin, making sure that every portion has some liquid. Divide the goat cheese into four pieces, and flatten each piece into a 2-inch (5 cm) disc. Place one disc on top of each pie.

8. Cover the filling and cheese with a sheet of crust, pinching the excess pastry to the outside edges of rims. Beat the egg and milk together and brush all over the crusts.

9. Bake for 20 to 22 minutes, until pie crusts are golden brown. Serve immediately with salad.

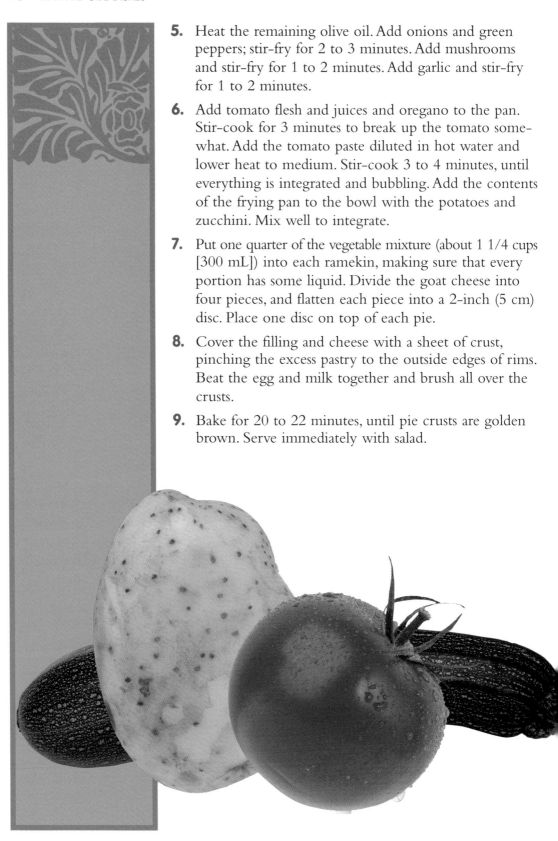

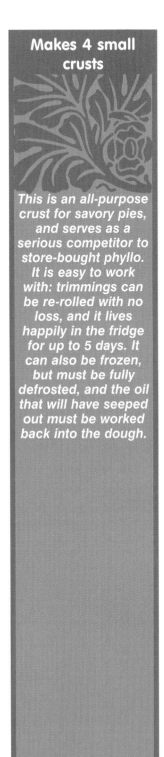

Makes 4 small crusts

This is an all-purpose crust for savory pies, and serves as a serious competitor to store-bought phyllo. It is easy to work with: trimmings can be re-rolled with no loss, and it lives happily in the fridge for up to 5 days. It can also be frozen, but must be fully defrosted, and the oil that will have seeped out must be worked back into the dough.

FROM
The New Vegetarian Gourmet
Byron Ayanoglu

Olive Oil Crust

1 3/4 cups	all-purpose flour	425 mL
1 1/2 tsp	salt	7 mL
1 1/2 tsp	baking powder	7 mL
1/2 cup	olive oil	125 mL
1/2 cup	milk	125 mL
1	whole egg, beaten	1
	Additional flour, as needed	

1. In a bowl, sift together the flour, salt and baking powder. In a separate bowl, whisk together olive oil, milk and beaten egg. Add the liquid ingredients all at once to the dry ingredients. Using fingers or an electric mixer with dough hook, blend the liquids into the flour. (If you use a mixer, scrape down the sides of the bowl several times.) This shouldn't take long; the dough will have absorbed the liquids and have the texture of an earlobe. If dough does not have the correct texture, work in another 2 tbsp (25 mL) flour.

2. Transfer the dough to a storage bowl, cover and refrigerate for at least 1/2 hour. When ready to use, knead any oil that may have seeped out back into the dough.

3. To roll crusts for making the pies in this book, divide the dough into 4 equal pieces. On a floured work surface, take one of the pieces of dough and flatten it into a round with your hand. Turn it over to flour the other side. Using a floured rolling pin, roll dough into a round sheet about 8 or 9 inches (19 or 22 cm) in diameter and about 1/8 inch (0.2 cm) thick. It will shrink a little on its own, but can be stretched by hand later. Transfer onto a piece of waxed paper. Repeat procedure for each of the 3 remaining pieces of dough, and stack them, separated by waxed paper, to ensure that they peel off easily when ready to use. The stack can then be covered and refrigerated.

T I P

Here's a great variation on the traditional omelet — but with less fat and cholesterol.

Replace beans and vegetables with other varieties of your choice.

Coriander can be replaced with dill, parsley and basil.

MAKE AHEAD

Combine entire mixture early in the day. Cook just before serving.

FROM
Rose Reisman's
Light Vegetarian Cooking

Black Bean, Corn and Leek Frittata

1 1/2 tsp	vegetable oil	7 mL
2 tsp	minced garlic	10 mL
3/4 cup	chopped leeks	175 mL
1/2 cup	chopped red bell peppers	125 mL
1/2 cup	canned or frozen corn kernels, drained	125 mL
1/2 cup	canned black beans, rinsed and drained	125 mL
1/3 cup	chopped fresh coriander	75 mL
2	eggs	2
3	egg whites	3
1/3 cup	2% milk	75 mL
1/4 tsp	salt	1 mL
1/4 tsp	freshly ground black pepper	1 mL
2 tbsp	grated Parmesan cheese	25 mL

1. In a nonstick saucepan sprayed with vegetable spray, heat oil over medium-high heat. Add garlic, leeks and red peppers; cook 4 minutes or until softened. Remove from heat; stir in corn, black beans and coriander.

2. In a bowl, whisk together whole eggs, egg whites, milk, salt and pepper. Stir in cooled vegetable mixture.

3. Spray a 12-inch (30 cm) nonstick frying pan with vegetable spray. Heat over medium-low heat. Pour in frittata mixture. Cook 5 minutes, gently lifting sides of frittata to let uncooked egg mixture flow under frittata. Sprinkle with Parmesan. Cover and cook another 3 minutes or until frittata is set. Slip frittata onto serving platter.

4. Cut into wedges and serve immediately

Serves 4 as a first course or 2 as a main course

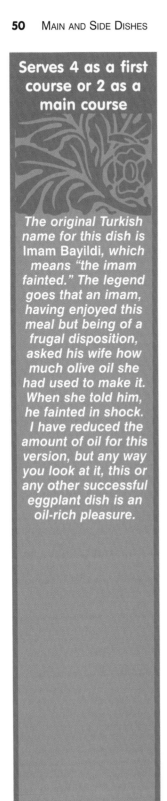

The original Turkish name for this dish is Imam Bayildi, which means "the imam fainted." The legend goes that an imam, having enjoyed this meal but being of a frugal disposition, asked his wife how much olive oil she had used to make it. When she told him, he fainted in shock. I have reduced the amount of oil for this version, but any way you look at it, this or any other successful eggplant dish is an oil-rich pleasure.

FROM
The New Vegetarian Gourmet
by Byron Ayanoglu

Individual Stuffed Eggplant

PREHEAT OVEN TO 400° F (210° C)
BAKING SHEET GREASED LIGHTLY WITH VEGETABLE OIL

2	small eggplants (about 2 by 4 inches [5 by 10 cm])	2
1 tsp	salt	5 mL
1/4 cup	vegetable oil	50 mL
3 tbsp	olive oil	45 mL
1/2 tsp	black pepper	2 mL
Pinch	cinnamon	Pinch
1	onion, finely diced	1
1/2	green pepper, cut into thin strips	1/2
3	cloves garlic, minced	3
1 tsp	dried oregano	5 mL
2 tbsp	currants *or* raisins	25 mL
1/4 cup	toasted pine nuts	50 mL
1	tomato, sliced	1
	Few sprigs fresh parsley, chopped	

1. Partially slice the eggplants lengthwise, without separating them, so they fan open, butterfly-like, skin-side down. Salt the flesh, and let stand for 10 minutes. Rinse them and pat dry.

2. In a large frying pan, heat vegetable oil over high heat until it's just about to smoke. Add the eggplants, flesh-side down — carefully: they'll splutter, so you may want to use a frying screen. Reduce heat to medium-high and fry for 2 minutes, until golden brown. Turn — again, carefully: more splutter — and fry the skin side for another 2 minutes. Remove from pan and set on paper towels to drain excess oil.

3. Discard any leftover oil from frying pan. Add olive oil and return to medium-high heat. Add black pepper and cinnamon and stir-fry for 30 seconds. Add diced onion and cook, stirring, for 2 minutes until the onion wilts. Add green pepper strips and stir-fry for 1 minute. Reduce heat to medium and add minced garlic, oregano and currants. Stir-fry for 2 minutes and remove from heat.

4. Spread the fried eggplants, skin-side down on baking sheet. Sprinkle the pine nuts evenly over the eggplants. Top evenly with the fried onion mixture and then the tomato slices. (This recipe can now wait for up to 1 hour, uncovered).

5. Bake the stuffed eggplants for 20 to 25 minutes until the tomatoes have baked down and everything looks shiny. Remove from oven and lift the eggplants carefully (to avoid breaking them) onto a serving platter. Garnish with chopped parsley and serve.

Cauliflower-Pea Curry

1 1/2 lbs	ripe tomatoes (about 6)	750 g
2	onions, quartered	2
5	cloves garlic, cut in half	5
2 tbsp	minced ginger root	25 mL
1 tbsp	turmeric	15 mL
1 tbsp	ground coriander	15 mL
2	hot green chilies, chopped	2
1/4 cup	ghee (clarified butter)	50 mL
1 tsp	black mustard seed	5 mL
1 tsp	whole cumin seed	5 mL
1 tsp	whole fennel seed	5 mL
1 tbsp	salt	15 mL
1	head cauliflower, florets only	1
3/4 cup	frozen peas	175 mL
1 tbsp	chopped fresh mint	15 mL
1 tsp	garam masala	5 mL
1/2 cup	yogurt	125 mL
2 tbsp	chopped fresh coriander	25 mL
	SPINACH DAL (see recipe, page 64)	
	Steamed rice	

1. Blanch tomatoes in boiling water for 30 seconds. Over a bowl, peel, core and deseed them. Chop tomatoes into chunks and set aside. Strain any accumulated tomato juices from bowl; add the juices to the tomatoes.

2. To the bowl of a food processor add onions, garlic, ginger, turmeric, coriander and chilies; process at high until thoroughly minced. Transfer mixture to a bowl.

3. Put tomatoes and tomato juices into the same food processor (you needn't bother washing it) and purée.

4. In a large saucepan, heat clarified butter over medium heat for 1 minute. Add the mustard, cumin and fennel seeds; stir-fry 2 to 3 minutes until the various seeds begin to pop. Add the reserved onion-garlic mixture and stir-fry until it all begins to darken, about 4 to 5 minutes. Add tomato purée and cook, stirring, for 5 minutes.

5. Stir salt and cauliflower into the sauce. Cook, uncovered, for 20 minutes, stirring occasionally.

6. Add frozen peas, mint and garam masala; fold together gently and cook for 3 to 4 minutes. Fold in yogurt and cook for 1 to 2 minutes; fold again and remove from heat. Let curry rest for a few minutes, uncovered. Transfer to a serving bowl and garnish generously with coriander. Serve with Spinach Dal and steamed rice.

Serves 4

Green Beans with Cashews

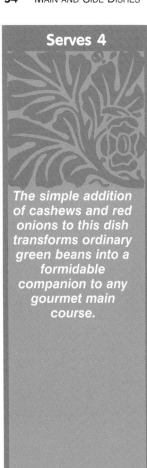

1 lb	green beans, trimmed	500 g
2 tbsp	olive oil	25 mL
1/2 cup	slivered red onions	125 mL
1/3 cup	raw cashews	75 mL
1/4 tsp	salt	1 mL
1/4 tsp	black pepper	1 mL
	Few sprigs fresh parsley, chopped	

The simple addition of cashews and red onions to this dish transforms ordinary green beans into a formidable companion to any gourmet main course.

1. Blanch green beans in a pot of boiling water for 5 minutes. Drain and immediately refresh in a bowl of ice-cold water. Drain and set aside.

2. In a large frying pan, heat olive oil over medium–high heat for 30 seconds. Add onions, cashews, salt and pepper and stir-fry for 2 to 3 minutes, until the onions are softened. Add cooked green beans, raise heat to high, and stir-fry actively for 2 to 3 minutes, until the beans feel hot to the touch. (Take care that you don't burn any cashews in the process.) Transfer to a serving plate and garnish with chopped parsley. Serve immediately.

FROM
The New Vegetarian Gourmet
by Byron Ayanoglu

FROM
Rose Reisman Brings
Home Light Cooking

Cauliflower, Broccoli and Goat Cheese Bake

Serves 4

TIP

Cut the cauliflower and broccoli into florets and 2-inch (5 cm) stem pieces.

The goat cheese can be replaced with mozzarella or Cheddar.

If in a hurry, omit the topping.

MAKE AHEAD

Sauce and topping can be prepared early in day. Warm sauce gently before pouring over vegetables. Add a little more milk to thin.

PREHEAT BROILER
BAKING DISH SPRAYED WITH NONSTICK VEGETABLE SPRAY

2 1/2 cups	chopped cauliflower	625 mL
2 1/2 cups	chopped broccoli	625 mL
1 tbsp	margarine	15 mL
1 tbsp	all-purpose flour	15 mL
1/2 cup	2% milk	125 mL
1/2 cup	chicken stock	125 mL
2 oz	goat cheese	50 g
2 tbsp	diced sweet red pepper	25 mL

Topping

1/3 cup	bran cereal★	75 mL
1 tsp	margarine, melted	5 mL
1/2 tsp	crushed garlic	2 mL

★ *Use a wheat bran breakfast cereal*

1. Steam or microwave cauliflower and broccoli until just tender. Drain and place in baking dish.

2. In small saucepan, melt margarine; add flour and cook, stirring, for 1 minute. Add milk and stock; cook, stirring continuously, until thickened, approximately 5 minutes. Remove from stove. Stir in goat cheese until melted; pour over vegetables. Sprinkle red pepper over top.

3. Topping: In food processor, combine cereal, margarine and garlic; process using on/off motion until crumbly. Sprinkle over vegetables. Broil until browned, approximately 2 minutes.

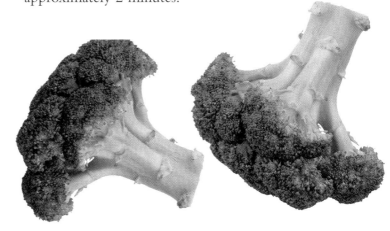

Eggplant Omelet with Filipino Tomato Salsa

Serves 2 as a main course or 4 to 6 as a shared course

This is a simple yet elegant dish that can be served as either a main course or a shared course in an Asian-style meal. The tomato sauce can be prepared well ahead of time, as can the roasting of the eggplant; final cooking is a matter of a few minutes. For a vegetarian version, simply replace fish sauce with salt. The recipe makes two 2-egg omelets.

The coriander in the tomato sauce can be replaced with another fresh herb, such as basil, mint or parsley.

In the Philippines there is a native herb that closely resembles parsley, with a hint of celery taste, known as *kintsay*; it can be replicated by mixing Italian (flat-leafed) parsley with Chinese celery or regular celery.

If you have leftover crab or lobster meat, it is delicious to spread the eggplant with the chopped meat before adding the egg.

FROM
The Asian Bistro Cookbook by Andrew Chase

2	Asian eggplants	2
1 cup	peeled, seeded and chopped ripe tomatoes	250 mL
4 tsp	olive oil	20 mL
1 tbsp	chopped coriander	15 mL
1 tbsp	fish sauce *or* 1 finely chopped anchovy and 1/4 tsp (1 mL) salt	15 mL
2 tsp	lime or lemon juice	10 mL
1 1/2 tsp	grated ginger root	7 mL
1/2 to 1 tsp	finely chopped chilies	2 to 5 mL
1/4 to 1/2 tsp	minced garlic	1 to 2 mL
1/4 tsp	black pepper	1 mL
1/4 tsp	salt	1 mL
1/8 tsp	granulated sugar	0.5 mL
1	shallot, minced	1
4	eggs	4
	Coriander sprigs for garnish	

1. Prick each eggplant in a few places with a fork. Bake in preheated 475° F (250° C) oven 20 minutes. Cool and peel, leaving stem attached. Flatten flesh out with the back of a fork.

2. In a bowl stir together tomatoes, 1 tsp (5 mL) of the olive oil, coriander, 2 tsp (10 mL) of the fish sauce, lime juice, ginger, chilies, garlic, 1/8 tsp (0.5 mL) of the pepper, salt, sugar and shallot; mix well.

3. Beat eggs with remaining fish sauce or 1/4 tsp (1 mL) salt and remaining pepper until well mixed but not frothy. In a small nonstick frying pan or omelet pan, heat half of remaining olive oil over medium heat; cook 1 eggplant for 30 seconds. Pour in half of egg mixture, lifting eggplant so egg can flow beneath it. Cook until egg is set and bottom is golden; turn and cook until other side is golden. Fold sides of omelet over the eggplant; transfer to warm serving platter. Repeat with remaining olive oil, eggplant and egg mixture. Spoon tomato salsa in thin lines over omelets; serve garnished with coriander.

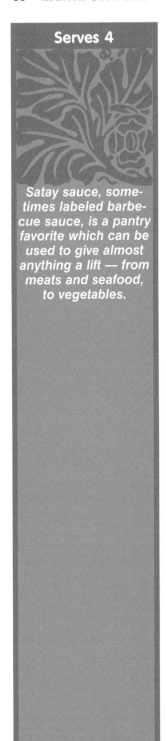

Satay sauce, sometimes labeled barbecue sauce, is a pantry favorite which can be used to give almost anything a lift — from meats and seafood, to vegetables.

FROM
New World Noodles
by Bill Jones & Stephen Wong

Satay-Glazed Vegetable Skewers with Cilantro Parmesan Noodles

PREHEAT BROILER OR, IF USING, START BARBECUE

2	zucchini, cut into a total of 16 slices, each 1 inch (2.5 cm) thick	2
2	red bell peppers, cut into a total of 16 large squares	2
16	large mushrooms	16
8	bamboo skewers, soaked in water for 4 hours	8
2 tbsp	olive oil	25 mL

Basting Sauce

1 tbsp	satay sauce (Chinese barbecue sauce)	15 mL
1 tbsp	honey	15 mL
1 tbsp	hoisin sauce	15 mL
1 tbsp	soya sauce	15 mL
1 tbsp	balsamic vinegar	15 mL
1	recipe CILANTRO PARMESAN NOODLES (see recipe, page 60)	1

1. Thread skewers in an attractive arrangement, using 2 pieces of each vegetable for each skewer.

2. In a small bowl, combine ingredients for basting sauce and mix well.

3. Prepare CILANTRO PARMESAN NOODLES and keep warm.

4. Brush vegetable skewers with olive oil and grill or broil 1 minute on each side. Baste each side with sauce and continue cooking for another 2 minutes on each side or until vegetables are just tender. Continue to baste during cooking to ensure that the vegetables are well coated and seasoned.

5. Divide CILANTRO PARMESAN NOODLES between 4 plates. Top with cooked vegetables; serve immediately.

Serves 4 as a
main course or 6
to 8 as a side dish

This quick and easy noodle dish is one of our standbys. Add a big, green salad (and some grilled chicken, if you wish) and you can have a delicious and nutritious dinner in less than 20 minutes.

Cilantro Parmesan Noodles

1 lb	fresh Shanghai noodles or fresh fettuccine	500 g
2 tbsp	whipping (35%) cream	25 mL
1/2 cup	freshly grated Parmesan cheese	125 mL
1/2 cup	chopped cilantro	125 mL
	Salt and pepper to taste	

1. In a large pot of boiling salted water, cook noodles until *al dente*, about 3 minutes. (If using pasta, prepare according to package instructions.) Drain.

2. Immediately return noodles to pot. Over low heat, add cream and Parmesan; mix. Add cilantro and toss thoroughly to combine. Season to taste with salt and pepper. Serve immediately.

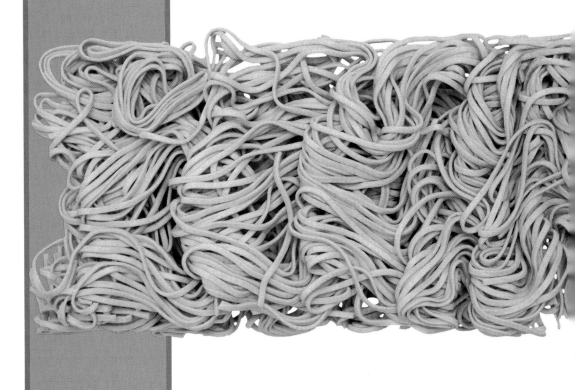

FROM
New World Noodles
by Bill Jones & Stephen Wong

Spinach with Cheddar Cheese Sauce and Crunchy Topping

PREHEAT BROILER
8- BY 4-INCH (1.5 L) BAKING DISH SPRAYED WITH VEGETABLE SPRAY

2	packages (10 oz [300 g]) frozen spinach	2
1 tsp	vegetable oil	5 mL
1 1/2 tsp	minced garlic	7 mL
3/4 cup	chopped onions	175 mL

Sauce

2 tsp	margarine or butter	10 mL
1 tbsp	all-purpose flour	15 mL
1/2 cup	chicken stock	125 mL
3/4 cup	2% milk	175 mL
2/3 cup	grated Cheddar cheese (2 1/2 oz [65 g])	150 mL

Topping

3 tbsp	seasoned bread crumbs	45 mL
1 tsp	minced garlic	5 mL
1 tsp	margarine or butter	5 mL

1. Cook spinach according to package directions; drain well and chop. Heat oil in nonstick skillet over medium heat; add garlic and onions and cook for 4 minutes or until softened. Toss with spinach and put in prepared baking dish.

2. Melt margarine in saucepan over medium heat; add flour and cook, stirring, for 1 minute. Gradually add stock and milk, stirring constantly. Cook until sauce begins to simmer and thickens slightly, approximately 5 minutes. Stir in cheese and cook 1 minute until cheese melts. Pour over spinach.

3. In a small bowl, combine bread crumbs, garlic, and margarine; sprinkle over sauce. Broil for 3 minutes or until browned.

Serves 4

TIP

For a change, substitute asparagus for the broccoli, and goat cheese for the feta.

Broccoli with Feta Cheese and Red Pepper

4 cups	chopped broccoli florets and 2-inch (5 cm) stalk pieces	1 L
2 tsp	vegetable oil	10 mL
2 tsp	crushed garlic	10 mL
3/4 cup	diced onions	175 mL
1/2 cup	diced red pepper	125 mL
1/3 cup	sliced black olives	75 mL
1 cup	diced tomatoes	250 mL
2 tbsp	chicken stock	25 mL
1 tsp	dried oregano (or 2 tbsp [25 mL] chopped fresh)	5 mL
1 1/2 oz	feta cheese, crumbled	40 g

1. Steam or microwave broccoli just until barely tender. Drain and set aside.

2. In nonstick skillet, heat oil; sauté garlic and onions just until softened, approximately 3 minutes. Add broccoli, olives, tomatoes, chicken stock and oregano; cook for 3 minutes. Place in serving dish. Sprinkle with feta cheese.

FROM
Rose Reisman Brings Home Light Cooking

Tomatoes Stuffed with Spinach and Ricotta Cheese

Serves 4

MAKE AHEAD

Make early in day and refrigerate. Bake just prior to serving.

PREHEAT OVEN TO 350° F (180° C)
BAKING DISH SPRAYED WITH VEGETABLE SPRAY

4 cups	fresh spinach	1 L
4	medium tomatoes	4
2 1/2 tsp	vegetable oil	12 mL
2 tsp	crushed garlic	10 mL
2/3 cup	chopped onions	150 mL
2/3 cup	ricotta cheese	150 mL
	Salt and pepper	

Topping

1 tbsp	dry bread crumbs	15 mL
1 tbsp	chopped fresh parsley	15 mL
1 tsp	margarine	5 mL
1 tsp	grated Parmesan cheese	5 mL

1. Rinse spinach and shake off excess water. With just the water clinging to leaves, cook until wilted. Squeeze out excess moisture; chop and set aside.

2. Slice off tops of tomatoes. Scoop out pulp, leaving shell of tomato intact. (Reserve pulp for another use.)

3. In a nonstick skillet, heat oil; sauté garlic and onions until softened. Remove from heat. Add spinach, cheese, and salt and pepper to taste; mix well. Fill tomatoes with cheese mixture and place in prepared baking dish.

4. Topping: Combine bread crumbs, parsley, margarine and cheese; sprinkle over tomatoes. Bake for 15 minutes or until heated through and topping is golden brown.

FROM
Rose Reisman Brings Home Light Cooking

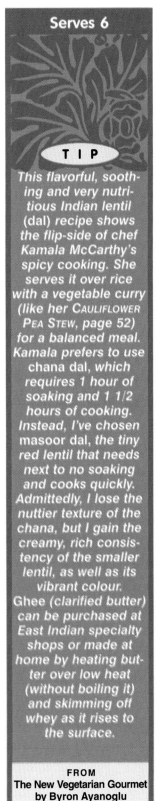

Serves 6

T I P

This flavorful, soothing and very nutritious Indian lentil (dal) recipe shows the flip-side of chef Kamala McCarthy's spicy cooking. She serves it over rice with a vegetable curry (like her CAULIFLOWER PEA STEW, page 52) for a balanced meal. Kamala prefers to use chana dal, which requires 1 hour of soaking and 1 1/2 hours of cooking. Instead, I've chosen masoor dal, the tiny red lentil that needs next to no soaking and cooks quickly. Admittedly, I lose the nuttier texture of the chana, but I gain the creamy, rich consistency of the smaller lentil, as well as its vibrant colour. Ghee (clarified butter) can be purchased at East Indian specialty shops or made at home by heating butter over low heat (without boiling it) and skimming off whey as it rises to the surface.

FROM
The New Vegetarian Gourmet
by Byron Ayanoglu

Spinach Dal

3 1/2 cups	*masoor dal* (red lentils), rinsed and drained	875 mL
8 cups	water	2 L
1 tbsp	turmeric	15 mL
1 tsp	whole cloves	5 mL
3	bay leaves	3
2 tbsp	*ghee* (clarified butter)	25 mL
2	onions, finely chopped	2
2 tbsp	minced ginger root	25 mL
5	cloves garlic, minced	5
6 cups	chopped fresh spinach, packed down	1.5 L
1 tbsp	salt	15 mL
1/4 cup	*ghee* (clarified butter)	50 mL
1 tsp	black mustard seeds	5 mL
1 tsp	whole cumin seeds	5 mL
4 tsp	*garam masala*	20 mL
2 tbsp	chopped fresh coriander	25 mL
	Steamed rice	

1. Put *dal* and water into a large pot and bring to a boil. Remove from heat. Add turmeric, cloves and bay leaves and stir. Let sit for 10 to 15 minutes until *dal* has swollen and has soaked up much of the water.

2. Place the lentil pot over high heat and cook for 5 to 7 minutes, stirring occasionally, until bubbling. Reduce heat to medium and cook for another 15 to 20 minutes, stirring occasionally, until the dal is tender. (If the *dal* dries out, add 1 or 2 cups [250 to 500 mL] boiling water.)

3. Meanwhile, in a frying pan heat the *ghee* over high heat for 30 seconds. Add onions and stir-fry for 2 minutes. Add ginger and garlic; stir-fry for another 2 minutes. Remove from heat and add to the *dal*. Continue cooking the *dal* with its new additions for 5 minutes, stirring occasionally. Add spinach strips and salt, stir well and cook for 10 minutes.

4. Meanwhile, in a small saucepan heat *ghee* over medium heat for 1 minute. Add the mustard and cumin seeds. Stir-fry for 2 to 3 minutes until the seeds begin to pop. Add this mixture to the simmering *dal*. The hot fat will hit the wet lentils with a distinct sizzle (this is called a "chaunk"). Stir, and add 3 tsp (45 mL) of the *garam masala*. Stir again, reduce heat to medium-low, and cook for 5 minutes, stirring occasionally.

5. Remove from heat and let rest uncovered for 15 minutes. Transfer to a serving bowl, sprinkle with the remaining *garam masala* and the coriander. Serve accompanied by CAULIFLOWER–PEA CURRY and steamed rice.

Serves 6

TIP

For a main course version, 4 oz (125 g) ground beef, veal or chicken can be added when the vegetables are sautéed. Serve 2 boats per person.

MAKE AHEAD

Prepare early in the day and refrigerate. Bake just before serving.

FROM
Rose Reisman Brings
Home Light Cooking

Zucchini Boats Stuffed with Cheese and Vegetables

PREHEAT OVEN TO 375° F (190° C)

3	medium zucchini	3
1 tbsp	vegetable oil	15 mL
2 tsp	crushed garlic	10 mL
1/2 cup	finely diced onions	125 mL
1/2 cup	finely diced mushrooms	125 mL
1/4 cup	finely diced sweet red pepper	50 mL
2 tbsp	chopped fresh dill (or 1 tsp [5 mL] dried)	25 mL
3 tbsp	dry bread crumbs	45 mL
4 tsp	grated Parmesan cheese	20 mL
	Salt and pepper	
1/4 cup	shredded mozzarella cheese	50 mL

1. Trim off ends of zucchini. Cook zucchini in boiling water for 3 minutes or until tender. Drain and rinse with cold water. Slice each lengthwise in half. With sharp knife, carefully remove pulp, leaving shell intact. Finely dice pulp and squeeze out excess moisture.

2. In a nonstick skillet, heat oil; sauté garlic, onions, mushrooms, red pepper and zucchini until softened, approximately 10 minutes. Add dill, bread crumbs, Parmesan, and salt and pepper to taste; mix well.

3. Spoon filling evenly into zucchini shells and place in baking dish. Top each with mozzarella. Bake for 10 minutes or until hot and cheese melts.

Pasta and Grains

Serves 4

TIP

Try Vidalia onions when in season (usually in the spring).

If using fresh basil, you'll get a more pronounced flavor if you add the basil after the pasta is tossed with the sauce. (Dried basil is added during the cooking.)

MAKE AHEAD

Cook onions 1 day in advance. Reheat, then continue recipe.

Linguine with Caramelized Onions, Tomatoes and Basil

2 tsp	vegetable oil	10 mL
2 tsp	minced garlic	10 mL
2 tbsp	packed brown sugar	25 mL
6 cups	thinly sliced red onions	1.5 L
2 cups	diced plum tomatoes	500 mL
3/4 cup	vegetable stock	175 mL
1/2 cup	chopped fresh basil	125 mL
	(or 1 1/2 tsp [7 mL] dried)	
1/4 tsp	freshly ground black pepper	1 mL
12 oz	linguine	375 g

1. In a large nonstick saucepan, heat oil over medium-low heat. Add garlic, sugar and red onions; cook, stirring often, 30 minutes or until browned and very soft.

2. Stir in tomatoes, stock, basil and pepper; cook 5 minutes longer or until heated through.

3. Meanwhile, in a pot of boiling water, cook linguine until tender but firm. Drain and toss with sauce.

FROM
**Rose Reisman's
Light Vegetarian Cooking**

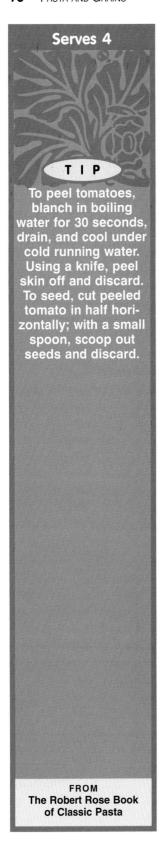

Serves 4

T I P

To peel tomatoes, blanch in boiling water for 30 seconds, drain, and cool under cold running water. Using a knife, peel skin off and discard. To seed, cut peeled tomato in half horizontally; with a small spoon, scoop out seeds and discard.

FROM
The Robert Rose Book of Classic Pasta

Penne with Zucchini and Eggplant

12 oz	penne	375 g
1/3 cup	olive oil	75 mL
1	clove garlic, crushed	1
8 oz	eggplant, cut in julienne strips	250 g
7 oz	zucchini, cut in julienne strips	210 g
1	large tomato, peeled, seeded and diced	1
2 tbsp	chopped fresh basil (or 1 tsp [5 mL] dried)	25 mL
5 oz	mozzarella cheese, preferably smoked, finely diced	150 g
	Salt and pepper to taste	

1. In a large pot of boiling salted water, cook penne 8 to 10 minutes or until *al dente*. Meanwhile, prepare the sauce.

2. In a skillet, heat oil over medium-high heat. Add garlic and cook until golden brown. Stir in eggplant and zucchini; cook 3 minutes. Stir in diced tomato and basil; cook 4 minutes longer. Add drained pasta and mix well. Stir in cheese; cook, stirring, until cheese begins to melt. Season to taste with salt and pepper. Serve immediately.

Fettuccine with Artichokes and Mushroom Sauce

Serves 4 to 6

TIP

Use canned drained artichoke hearts, or cook your own. To cook artichoke hearts: trim the leaves and choke from 10 artichokes, in a saucepan melt 2 tsp (10 mL) butter over medium heat, and sauté artichoke hearts until tender when pierced with the tip of a knife.

10	artichoke hearts (fresh cooked or canned, drained)	10
1/4 cup	vegetable oil	50 mL
1/2 lb	mushrooms, chopped	250 g
1/2 tsp	minced garlic	2 mL
1/4 cup	dry white wine	50 mL
1 1/2 cups	whipping (35%) cream	375 mL
1/2 tsp	ground saffron	2 mL
1 lb	fettuccine	500 g
1/3 cup	grated Parmesan cheese	75 mL
	Salt and pepper to taste	
	Fresh parsley sprigs	

1. Chop 6 of the artichoke hearts; set aside.

2. In a large skillet, heat oil over medium-high heat. Add mushrooms and garlic; cook 5 minutes. Add chopped artichokes and wine; cook 2 minutes. Stir in cream; bring to a boil. Stir in saffron, reduce heat to low and simmer 5 minutes.

3. Meanwhile, in a large pot of boiling salted water, cook fettuccine 8 to 10 minutes or until *al dente*; drain.

4. Toss pasta with artichoke sauce and Parmesan. Season to taste with salt and pepper. Serve immediately, garnished with whole artichoke hearts and parsley.

FROM
The Robert Rose Book
of Classic Pasta

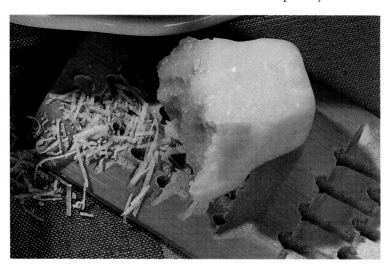

Serves 4

TIP

This can be served either warm or cold.

Instead of zucchini, try chopped broccoli.

Try goat cheese instead of feta for a change.

MAKE AHEAD

Prepare and refrigerate early in day. Reheat gently until just warm. If serving cold, stir well before serving.

FROM
Rose Reisman Brings Home Light Cooking

Spicy Rice with Feta Cheese and Black Olives

1 tbsp	vegetable oil	15 mL
2 tsp	crushed garlic	10 mL
1/2 cup	chopped onions	125 mL
1/2 cup	chopped zucchini	125 mL
1/4 cup	chopped sweet red pepper	50 mL
1 cup	rice	250 mL
1 1/2 cups	chicken stock	375 mL
1 tsp	dried oregano	5 mL
1 tsp	dried basil	5 mL
1 tsp	chili powder	5 mL
1/4 cup	sliced pitted black olives	50 mL
2 oz	feta cheese, crumbled	50 g

1. In a large nonstick saucepan, heat oil; sauté garlic, onions, zucchini and red pepper until softened, approximately 5 minutes. Add rice and brown for 2 minutes, stirring constantly.

2. Add stock, oregano, basil, chili powder and olives; cover and simmer for approximately 20 minutes or until rice is tender. Pour into serving dish and sprinkle with cheese.

Pasta with Fresh Spring Vegetables and Mint

12 oz	angel hair pasta (fine strand)	375 g
1 tbsp	olive oil	15 mL
2 tsp	crushed garlic	10 mL
4 oz	chopped snow peas	125 g
1 cup	diced zucchini	250 mL
1	small carrot, finely diced	1
1 cup	finely diced sweet red peppers	250 mL
1 cup	frozen green peas	250 mL
2 1/2 cups	cold chicken stock *or* vegetable stock	625 mL
2 tbsp + 2 tsp	all-purpose flour	35 mL
1/2 cup	chopped fresh mint (or 1 1/2 tsp [7 mL] dried)	125 mL

1. Cook pasta in boiling water according to package instructions or until firm to the bite. Drain and place in serving bowl.

2. In large nonstick skillet, heat oil; sauté garlic, snow peas, zucchini, carrot and red peppers until just tender, for 5 to 8 minutes. Add peas and sauté for 2 minutes.

3. Meanwhile, in small bowl, combine stock with flour until smooth. Add to vegetables and simmer just until slightly thickened, approximately 4 minutes, stirring constantly. Add mint and pour over pasta. Toss.

Wild Rice with Sautéed Oriental Vegetables

1 tbsp	margarine	15 mL
1/2 cup	chopped onions	125 mL
1 tsp	crushed garlic	5 mL
1/3 cup	wild rice	75 mL
1/3 cup	white rice	75 mL
1 3/4 cups	chicken stock	425 mL
1/2 cup	chopped broccoli	125 mL
1/2 cup	chopped sweet red pepper	125 mL
1 cup	snow peas, cut in half	250 mL
2 tbsp	chicken stock	25 mL
2 1/2 tsp	soya sauce	12 mL
2 tbsp	sliced almonds, toasted	25 mL
1/4 cup	chopped green onions	50 mL

1. In medium nonstick saucepan, melt half of the margarine; sauté onions and garlic for 3 minutes or until softened. Add wild and white rice; sauté just until golden, approximately 3 minutes.

2. Add 1 3/4 cups (425 mL) stock; cover and simmer for approximately 40 minutes or just until rice is tender and liquid absorbed, adding more stock if mixture dries out too quickly. Place in serving bowl.

3. In large nonstick skillet, melt remaining margarine; sauté broccoli, red pepper and snow peas just until tender-crisp. Add remaining 2 tbsp (25 mL) stock and soya sauce; cook for 1 minute. Pour over rice and mix well. Sprinkle with almonds and green onions.

Baked Rice Noodle Rolls with Mushrooms, Olives and a Herbed Tomato Sauce

PREHEAT OVEN TO 350° F (180° C)
9- BY 13-INCH (3 L) OVENPROOF CASSEROLE DISH
GREASED WITH OLIVE OIL

1	can (28 oz [796 mL]) tomatoes	1
2 tbsp	olive oil *or* vegetable oil	25 mL
1	onion, diced	1
2 cups	sliced mushrooms	500 mL
2	cloves garlic, minced	2
1/4 cup	pitted, coarsely chopped green olives	50 mL
1 tbsp	chopped fresh marjoram (or 1/2 tsp [2 mL] dried)	15 mL
1 tbsp	chopped rosemary (fresh or dried) Salt and pepper to taste	15 mL
1 lb	fresh rice noodle rolls *or* cooked lasagna sheets	500 g
2 cups	shredded skim mozzarella cheese	500 mL

1. In a medium-sized bowl, crush tomatoes with a fork (or pulse in a food processor) until they are in bite-size pieces. Set aside.

2. In a nonstick wok or skillet, heat oil over medium-high heat for 30 seconds. Add onions and sauté until they begin to color. Add mushrooms and garlic and cook until mushrooms begin to soften. Stir in tomatoes, olives, marjoram and rosemary; season with salt and pepper and bring to a simmer. Cook for 3 minutes.

3. Spread 1/4 cup (50 mL) of sauce evenly over bottom of prepared dish, then unroll 3 noodle sheets over sauce. Top with one third of the sauce and an equal amount of cheese. Repeat with remaining sauce and sheets until you have 3 layers. Bake for 30 minutes or until top is golden brown. Let rest for 3 to 4 minutes before serving.

FROM
New World Noodles
by Bill Jones & Stephen Wong

Makes 10 cakes

Rice Cakes with Tomato Purée

T I P

Serve these with soup and salad for an excellent complete meal. Or serve as a side dish.

These cakes can also be sautéed in a non-stick skillet sprayed with vegetable spray.

Try brown rice. Cook 35 minutes or until tender, adding more stock if necessary.

MAKE AHEAD

Prepare cakes up to 1 day in advance; keep refrigerated until ready to bake.

PREHEAT OVEN TO 425° F (220° C)
BAKING SHEET SPRAYED WITH VEGETABLE SPRAY

Rice Cakes

4 cups	vegetable stock	1 L
1/2 cup	wild rice	125 mL
1/2 cup	white rice	125 mL
1 tsp	minced garlic	5 mL
1/2 cup	shredded part-skim mozzarella cheese (about 2 oz [50 g])	125 mL
1/4 cup	shredded Swiss cheese (about 1/2 oz [15 g])	50 mL
1/4 cup	chopped green onions	50 mL
2 tbsp	grated Parmesan cheese	25 mL
1 tsp	dried basil	5 mL
1	egg	1
2	egg whites	2

Sauce

1/2 cup	prepared tomato pasta sauce	125 mL
2 tbsp	2% milk	25 mL
1/4 tsp	dried basil	1 mL

1. In a saucepan, bring stock to a boil; stir in wild rice and white rice; cover, reduce heat to medium-low and cook 35 minutes or until rice is tender. Let rice cool slightly. Drain any excess liquid. Rinse with cold water.

2. In a bowl, stir together cooled rice, garlic, mozzarella, Swiss, green onions, Parmesan, basil, whole egg and egg whites until well mixed. Using a 1/4 cup (50 mL) measure, form mixture into 10 patties.

3. Place on prepared baking sheet. Bake approximately 10 minutes per side until browned.

4. Meanwhile, in a small saucepan, heat tomato sauce, milk and basil. Serve with rice cakes.

FROM
Rose Reisman's
Light Vegetarian Cooking

Serves 6 to 8

TIP

Polenta is an excellent choice for a vegetarian main meal. It's delicious and nutritious.

To soften sun-dried tomatoes, pour boiling water over them and soak 15 minutes or until soft. Drain and chop.

MAKE AHEAD

Prepare to end of Step 3 earlier in day. Bring sauce back to a simmer before proceeding with Step 4.

FROM
**Rose Reisman's
Light Vegetarian Cooking**

Polenta Cubes with Goat Cheese Vegetable Sauce

13- BY 9-INCH (3 L) BAKING DISH SPRAYED WITH VEGETABLE SPRAY

Polenta Cubes

4 cups	vegetable stock	1 L
2 cups	cornmeal	500 mL
1/8 tsp	cayenne pepper	0.5 mL
2 tbsp	grated Parmesan cheese	25 mL
1 1/2 tsp	minced garlic	7 mL

Sauce

2 tsp	vegetable oil	10 mL
2 tsp	minced garlic	10 mL
2 cups	chopped leeks	500 mL
2 cups	chopped red bell peppers	500 mL
1 1/2 cups	vegetable stock	375 mL
2/3 cup	chopped softened sun-dried tomatoes (see Tip, at left)	150 mL
1/2 cup	sliced black olives	125 mL
2 tsp	dried basil	10 mL
4 oz	goat cheese, crumbled	125 g
2 tbsp	balsamic vinegar	25 mL

1. In a deep saucepan, bring vegetable stock to a boil. Reduce heat to low and gradually whisk in cornmeal and cayenne pepper. Cook 5 minutes, stirring frequently. Stir in Parmesan and garlic. Spoon into prepared baking dish, using the back of a wet spoon to smooth top. Cover and chill while making sauce.

2. In a large nonstick saucepan sprayed with vegetable spray, heat oil over medium-high heat. Add garlic, leeks and red peppers; cook 5 to 8 minutes until soft and slightly browned. Stir in vegetable stock, sun-dried tomatoes, olives and basil; reduce heat to medium, cover and cook 4 minutes.

3. Meanwhile, turn cooled polenta onto a cutting board. Cut into 1/2-inch (1 cm) squares.

4. Stir goat cheese and vinegar into sauce until cheese melts. Stir in polenta cubes; cook, stirring, 4 minutes or until heated through. Serve immediately.

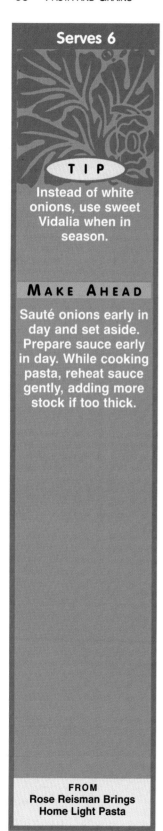

Serves 6

TIP

Instead of white onions, use sweet Vidalia when in season.

MAKE AHEAD

Sauté onions early in day and set aside. Prepare sauce early in day. While cooking pasta, reheat sauce gently, adding more stock if too thick.

FROM
Rose Reisman Brings Home Light Pasta

Rotini with Three-Onion and Garlic Sauce

12 oz	rotini	375 g
1 tbsp	vegetable oil	15 mL
2 tsp	crushed garlic	10 mL
2 cups	sliced red onions	500 mL
2 cups	sliced white onions	500 mL
1 1/2 cups	chopped green onions	375 mL
1 tbsp	margarine or butter	15 mL
2 tbsp + 1 tsp	all-purpose flour	35 mL
1 cup	chicken stock *or* vegetable stock	250 mL
1 cup	2% milk	250 mL
1/4 cup	dry white wine	50 mL
Dash	nutmeg	Dash
1/4 cup	grated Parmesan cheese	50 mL

1. Cook pasta in boiling water according to package instructions or until firm to the bite. Drain and place in serving bowl.

2. In large nonstick skillet sprayed with vegetable spray, heat oil; sauté garlic and red, white and green onions, until tender, approximately 7 minutes. Add to pasta.

3. In medium nonstick saucepan, melt margarine; add flour and cook for 1 minute. Slowly add chicken stock, milk and wine. Stir constantly over medium heat, just until slightly thickened, approximately 4 minutes. Add nutmeg. Pour over pasta. Sprinkle with cheese, and toss.

Desserts

Serves 6

T I P

Frozen strawberries can be used if fresh ones are out of season. Be sure to check sweetness before adding honey as some frozen berries may already have sugar added.

Candied ginger is usually sold in a jar with syrup, but we have seen it in semi-dried form, coated in sugar. If that's the kind you're using, substitute ginger juice and honey for the syrup.

To make ginger juice: In a food processor or chopper, purée 8 thick slices of ginger root and 1 tbsp (15 mL) water. Extract juice by pushing pulp through a very fine sieve.

FROM
New World Chinese Cooking
by Bill Jones & Stephen Wong

Candied Ginger and Strawberry Parfait

2 tbsp	minced candied ginger	25 mL
1 tsp	ginger juice (see Tip, at left)	5 mL
1 tbsp	syrup from candied ginger *or* 1 tbsp (15 mL) ginger juice, sweetened with 1 tsp (5 mL) honey	15 mL
2 cups	sliced strawberries	500 mL
	Maple syrup, to taste	
2 cups	vanilla ice cream	500 mL
1 cup	whipped cream	250 mL

1. In a bowl combine ginger, ginger juice, syrup and strawberries; mix well. Adjust sweetness with maple syrup and set aside to marinate for 20 minutes.

2. To serve: Place about 2 tbsp (25 mL) strawberry mixture in the bottom of a parfait glass. Add 2 tbsp (25 mL) ice cream; repeat layers until parfait glass is filled. Top with a dollop of whipped cream and serve immediately.

FROM
The Asian Bistro Cookbook
by Andrew Chase

Serves 4

T I P

This dessert is inspired by a snack sold from street stalls everywhere in the Philippines. It is a simple dish that goes very well with ice cream, particularly vanilla or caramel. Small bananas (sometimes mistakenly sold as "baby bananas"), regular large bananas or red ones, are all good here.

Use the large-size, commercially produced spring or egg roll wrappers. You can substitute the more readily available 5-inch (12 cm) square egg roll wrappers; with a rolling pin, roll them as thin as possible and proceed with recipe.

Variation
Try adding 1/2 cup (125 mL) chopped nuts or 1 1/2 tbsp (20 mL) toasted sesame seeds.

Banana and Chocolate Spring Rolls

4	large spring roll wrappers (approximately 9 inches [22.5 cm] square)	4
4	small or 2 large bananas, cut in half crosswise	4
1/2 cup	grated semi-sweet chocolate	125 mL
2 tbsp	crystallized ginger cut into thin slivers (optional)	25 mL
1 tsp	cornstarch dissolved in 1 tsp (5 mL) water	5 mL
2 cups	vegetable oil	500 mL
2 tsp	icing sugar	10 mL

1. Lay the spring roll wrapper flat with one corner facing you; put banana across bottom third and sprinkle with one-quarter of the chocolate and ginger if desired. Roll up, tightly tucking in the sides, and seal with the cornstarch mixture (make sure there are no leaks in the wrapping). Repeat for each banana.

2. In wok or deep saucepan, heat oil to 350° F (180° C). Cook spring rolls until golden and crispy, turning once, about 90 seconds. Drain on paper towels. Serve warm or at room temperature, sprinkled with sifted icing sugar. Serve alone or with ice cream, whipped cream, or COCONUT CUSTARD CREAM (see following recipe).

Coconut Custard Cream

6	egg yolks	6
1/2 cup	granulated sugar	125 mL
1	can (14 oz [400 mL]) coconut milk	1
1/2 cup	milk	125 mL
2	green or white cardamom pods, slightly crushed	2
1	clove	1
1/4 tsp	vanilla extract	1 mL
1/8 tsp	salt	0.5 mL

1. Make the custard: In a bowl with an electric mixer, beat yolks with sugar until light-colored and forming ribbons. In a saucepan, combine coconut milk, milk, cardamom pods, clove, vanilla and salt; simmer slowly for 20 minutes. Gradually beat hot (but not boiling) coconut milk mixture into the egg yolk mixture. Return to pot and cook over low heat, stirring constantly, until thick enough to coat a spoon (do not boil). Strain immediately through a fine sieve; stir for 2 to 3 minutes as it cools to prevent curdling. Refrigerate after the custard has reached room temperature.

Serves 6 to 8

The crispy, warm wontons contrast with the smooth, cool ice cream, making this a luscious dessert. If you're not having yams with your holiday dinner, this would add a new twist to a traditional Christmas or Thanksgiving feast.

Hazelnut Yam Wonton with Maple Syrup

PREHEAT OVEN TO 200° F (95° C)

2 tbsp	butter	25 mL
1 tbsp	brown sugar	15 mL
1 tsp	cinnamon	5 mL
Pinch	nutmeg	Pinch
1	yam, roasted, skinned and mashed	1
1/2 cup	coarsely chopped roasted hazelnuts	125 mL
24	square wonton wrappers	24
1 cup	vegetable oil for frying	250 mL
2 tbsp	maple syrup	25 mL
2 tsp	icing sugar for garnish	10 mL
2 cups	vanilla ice cream, divided into 6 portions	500 mL

1. In a small skillet or saucepan, melt butter over low heat. Remove from heat, add sugar and spices; mix well.

2. In a mixing bowl, combine yam and nuts. Add half butter mixture and mix well.

3. On a work surface, lay out 1 wonton wrapper. Place 1 tbsp (15 mL) filling in center. Brush the edges with remaining butter mixture. Cover with another wonton wrapper, squeeze the air out by pressing with your fingertips and press edges together to seal. Repeat with remaining ingredients until all the filling is used. (You should be able to make 12 wontons.)

4. In a small pot, heat oil until a small piece of wonton wrapper sizzles and immediately floats to the top. Fry wontons one or two at a time until golden, about 20 seconds per side. Place finished wontons on paper towels to drain any excess oil. Keep warm in oven.

5. To serve, place 2 or 3 wontons on each plate, drizzle with maple syrup and dust with icing sugar. Serve vanilla ice cream as an accompaniment.

FROM
New World Noodles
by Bill Jones & Stephen Wong

Serves 12

T I P

Use vanilla wafer crumbs, or any dry cookie of your choice for the crust. Use food processor to break up whole cookies until they are crumbly.

Toast almonds in nonstick skillet on top of stove for 2 minutes until browned.

MAKE AHEAD

Bake up to 2 days ahead or freeze for up to 6 weeks. Tastes great even after 2 days in the refrigerator.

FROM
Rose Reisman's
Enlightened Home Cooking

Apple Cinnamon Cheesecake

PREHEAT OVEN TO 350° F (180° C)
8-INCH (2 L) SPRINGFORM PAN SPRAYED WITH VEGETABLE SPRAY

Crust

1 1/2 cups	graham cracker crumbs	375 mL
2 tbsp	granulated sugar	25 mL
2 tbsp	water	25 mL
1 tbsp	melted margarine or butter	15 mL
1/2 tsp	cinnamon	2 mL

Cake

1 cup	5% ricotta cheese	250 mL
1 cup	2% cottage cheese	250 mL
3/4 cup	granulated sugar	175 mL
3 tbsp	all-purpose flour	45 mL
1	egg	1
2 tsp	cinnamon	10 mL
1 1/2 tsp	vanilla	7 mL
1/4 tsp	almond extract	1 mL
1/2 cup	peeled, diced apples	125 mL

Topping

1 cup	light (1%) sour cream	250 mL
2 tbsp	granulated sugar	25 mL
1 tsp	vanilla	5 mL
1 tbsp	sliced toasted almonds	15 mL

1. In bowl, combine graham cracker crumbs, sugar, water, margarine and cinnamon; mix well. Press onto bottom and sides of springform pan; refrigerate.

2. Put ricotta cheese, cottage cheese, sugar, 2 tbsp (25 mL) of the flour, egg, 1 tsp (5 mL) of the cinnamon, vanilla and almond extract in food processor; process until smooth. In small bowl, combine remaining 1 tbsp (15 mL) flour and remaining 1 tsp (5 mL) cinnamon with apples. Stir apple mixture into batter. Pour into pan and bake for 25 minutes or until set around edges but still slightly loose at center.

3. Meanwhile, in small bowl, stir together sour cream, sugar and vanilla; pour over cheesecake and sprinkle with nuts. Return to oven and bake for 10 minutes longer. Topping will be loose. Let cool and refrigerate for 3 hours or overnight.

Serves 6 to 8

TIP

Blueberries should be removed from their carton and placed in a moisture-proof container in the refrigerator. Do not wash until just before using.

Other fresh, ripe fruit such as apples and pears are excellent variations.

MAKE AHEAD

Although best straight from the oven, crisp can be prepared early in the day and reheated slightly before serving.

FROM
Rose Reisman Brings
Home Light Cooking

Peach and Blueberry Crisp

PREHEAT OVEN TO 350° F (180° C)
9-INCH (2.5 L) SQUARE CAKE PAN

1/2 cup	granulated sugar	125 mL
2 tbsp	all-purpose flour	25 mL
2 tsp	lemon juice	10 mL
1 tsp	grated lemon rind	5 mL
1 tsp	cinnamon	5 mL
3 cups	sliced peeled ripe peaches	750 mL
2 cups	blueberries	500 mL

Topping

1/2 cup	rolled oats	125 mL
1/3 cup	all-purpose flour	75 mL
3 tbsp	brown sugar	45 mL
1/2 tsp	cinnamon	2 mL
3 tbsp	soft margarine	45 mL

1. In large bowl, combine sugar, flour, lemon juice, rind and cinnamon; stir in peaches and blueberries until well mixed. Spread in cake pan.

2. Topping: In small bowl, combine rolled oats, flour, sugar and cinnamon; cut in margarine until crumbly. Sprinkle over fruit. Bake for 30 to 35 minutes or until topping is browned and fruit is tender. Serve warm.

Index

If you've enjoyed the recipes in our "favorite" series, try our bestselling full-sized cookbooks.

Here's the book that established author Rose Reisman as a major force in the world of cookbook publishing. Now with more than 200,000 copies sold, *Light Cooking* proves that healthy eating doesn't have to be dull.
ISBN 1-896503-00-4

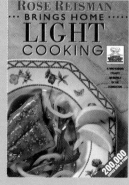

Everyone loves pasta. And here bestselling author Rose Reisman has created over 175 deliciously light pasta recipes. You won't believe how these pasta dishes can be so low in fat and calories — yet so full of flavor.
ISBN 1-896503-02-0

Everyone wants to provide their families with healthy, delicious meals. But these days, who has the time? You do! And Rose Reisman proves it in this collection of 175 light and easy recipes — all low in fat but full of taste.
ISBN 1-896503-12-8

Here's vegetarian cooking as only Rose Reisman can do it — imaginative, delicious and, unlike many vegetarian dishes, low in fat. A great book for today's families, with special appeal for "occasional vegetarians" who just want healthier meals.
ISBN 1-896503-66-7

Here's the ultimate book for pasta lovers, with over 100 recipes specially selected from the menus of top North American restaurants and adapted for home cooking. They're as simple to make as they are delicious. A must for every kitchen.
ISBN 1-896503-03-9

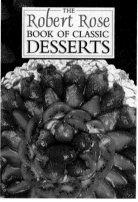

Go ahead — indulge yourself! Here's the ultimate collection of after-dinner delights, specially selected from the offerings of North America's top dessert chefs and adapted for home cooking. Over 100 recipes for the most scrumptiously satisfying desserts ever.
ISBN 1-896503-11-X

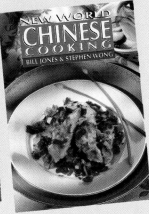

More of your favorite recipes

Just about everyone loves pasta. After all, there are few types of food that can be prepared in so many interesting ways. And that's what you'll discover in this book — over 50 pasta recipes, from classic comfort foods like macaroni and cheese to more exotic Asian-inspired noodle dishes.
ISBN 1-896503-74-8

Here's a book for all the people who love desserts, but worry about the fat and calories. Imagine being able to indulge, guilt-free, in luscious cheesecakes, pies — even chocolate desserts! Well, now you can. Over 50 great recipes with less than 200 calories per serving.
ISBN 1-896503-72-1

Guaranteed to satisfy everyone's sweet tooth, this collection features more than 50 of our best dessert recipes. Here you'll find a variety of scrumptious treats for just about any occasion. These recipes are delicious and easy to prepare — a delight for anyone who loves desserts.
ISBN 1-896503-71-3

Want something quick, easy and delicious? Then here's the book for you. Whether it's snacks for your kids, a light salad for lunch, or appetizers for dinner-party guests, you'll find just the right thing in this collection of 50 great recipes. They're winners every time.
ISBN 1-896503-51-9

Call it the most comforting type of comfort food — nothing beats a big bowl of hot soup or stew for pure, old-fashioned satisfaction. Here are over 50 outstanding recipes for these one-pot wonders. This book will be a popular addition to every family's kitchen.
ISBN 1-896503-72-1

What can you serve at mealtime that's guaranteed to please just about everyone? Chicken, of course! After all, chicken is lean and healthy; it's affordable and it's tremendously versatile. Here you get more than 50 terrific chicken recipes. A must for anyone who loves chicken.
ISBN 1-896503-53-5